Cognitive Styles
in Infancy and Early Childhood

Cognitive Styles
in Infancy
and Early Childhood

NATHAN KOGAN

GRADUATE FACULTY
NEW SCHOOL FOR SOCIAL RESEARCH

 LAWRENCE ERLBAUM ASSOCIATES, PUBLISHERS
1976　Hillsdale, New Jersey

DISTRIBUTED BY THE HALSTED PRESS DIVISION OF

JOHN WILEY & SONS

New York　Toronto　London　Sydney

Lawrence Erlbaum Associates, Inc., Publishers
62 Maria Drive
Hillsdale, New Jersey 07642

Distributed solely by Halsted Press Division
John Wiley & Sons, Inc., New York

Library of Congress Cataloging in Publication Data

Kogan, Nathan.
   Cognitive styles in infancy and early childhood.

   Bibliography: p.
   Includes index.
   1. Cognition (Child psychology) 2. Cognitive styles. 3. Infant psychology. I. Title.
BF723.C5K64   155.4'13   76-18926
ISBN 0-470-15149-8

Printed in the United States of America

Contents

Preface

Within almost any specialized area of psychology, a period of intensive research activity is eventually followed by an integrated and critical review, taking stock of what has been accomplished. Where the field is reasonably circumscribed, such reviews either make their way into the appropriate scholarly journals or appear as chapters in handbooks or other kinds of edited volumes. There are times, however, when the domain of interest has achieved so wide a scope that nothing short of monographic treatment can do adequate justice to it. This is clearly the current state of affairs in respect to the area of cognitive styles.

In the course of the past five years, I have been the author or coauthor of three separate book chapters devoted to cognitive styles in whole or in part (see Chapter 1). The first of these chapters concerned cognitive-style research in school-age children, the second focused on educational implications, and the third examined cognitive styles from a life-span perspective, with particular emphasis on the adult period.

Given this prior work, I should not have been surprised when Michael Lewis phoned me in January 1974 to ask whether I would be interested in contributing a chapter on cognitive styles in infancy and early childhood to a volume on *Origins of Intelligence* that he was editing for Plenum. I had, after all, been doing research on and writing extensively about cognitive styles for quite a few years. Nevertheless, I was in fact surprised by Dr. Lewis' invitation and rather reluctant to accept it. There were obvious reasons for this reluctance on my part. Only a minute portion of my own research was based on children of preschool age, and so it seemed a bit presumptuous to undertake an authoritative review based on age groups with which I had had such limited research experience. There was an even more practical reason, however, for my great hesitation. Although I was aware of a small number of studies concerned with cognitive styles in early childhood, I honestly did not believe at the time that the amount of available empirical information was sufficient to warrant the preparation of a book chapter.

After a considerable period of stalling, I officially signed the contract with the private expectation that my prospective chapter would hold the distinction of being the briefest in the volume. I accepted the assignment for two reasons. First, there was an obvious gap in my earlier reviews of the cognitive-style literature, for little effort had been made to examine the relevance of cognitive-style constructs for the period of early childhood. Even less attention had been devoted to the issue of precursors of cognitive styles in infancy. Although there did not appear to be much worth saying about these topics at the time of my decision to embark on the chapter, a case could be made for a review and critique of the limited available information, if only for the sake of a sense of closure. With the age of the various cognitive-style constructs ranging from approximately 10 (reflection-impulsivity) to 25 years (field independence-dependence), the time appeared to be ripe for a consideration of developmental origins.

My other reason for accepting an invitation to write the chapter is more personal in nature. At the risk of sounding trite, I must confess that the opportunity to explore a relatively uncharted domain posed an intellectual challenge. Although I was highly familiar with most aspects of cognitive styles, I had given little thought to their relevance for the earliest portion of the life span. The prospective chapter thus offered the potential of enlarging my own understanding of the area.

My original intention was to complete the chapter during the summer of 1974. I anticipated that it would be possible to read everything relevant to the topic in the preceding spring and so be possible for me to finish the job before the onset of fall and actually ahead of the editor's deadline. As the summer approached, it became strikingly clear that the published material would not be sufficient for a truly up-to-date contribution.

Approximately two years earlier, I had participated in an NIMH-sponsored conference on self-regulatory processes arranged by Jack Block and held in La Jolla, California. At that conference, Jeanne Block presented some preliminary findings from a massive research project on cognitive and personality processes in preschool children. Cognitive-style measures were included in that work, although the conference paper did not emphasize them. After an exchange of letters, it was clear to me that Jack and Jeanne Block had collected and analyzed a huge amount of data on preschoolers' cognitive styles. Most of this material had not at that time found its way into printed reports. It was clear that a visit to the University of California in Berkeley would be essential to assimilate the research that the Blocks had been pursuring for several years. An invitation to visit was graciously extended to me by Jack and Jeanne Block and, as a result, I spent a week in Tolman Hall in June 1974 trying to absorb as much as I could of the aims, procedures, and findings of the research in which they had been engaged for a number of years.

The visit to Berkeley dramatically expanded the scope of the intended chapter. Suddenly, I found myself in possession of a vast quantity of highly relevant unpublished findings. The Blocks also informed me of Susan Coates' research on field independence-dependence in preschoolers being carried out at the Downstate Medical Center of the State University of New York. Communication with Ms. Coates yielded a highly useful set of published and unpublished materials. Finally, I traveled to my former place of employment, Educational Testing Service in Princeton, and acquired the unpublished technical reports of the ETS Longitudinal Study authored by Virginia Shipman and William C. Ward.

Armed with all of the foregoing materials, I journeyed to Maine early in July 1974 fully expecting to produce a completed manuscript within two months. By the time the end of the summer arrived, it was quite obvious that I had seriously misjudged the scope of the task. Although I had produced approximately 65 pages of manuscript, its completion was clearly a long way off. The return to New York City and my traditional academic duties slowed me down considerably, but I continued to plug away at the manuscript hoping all along that Michael Lewis would be willing to tolerate a contribution somewhat longer than the typical chapter. By January 1975, the pretense of working on a chapter could no longer be sustained. The manuscript was running well over 100 pages, and coverage of the area was not yet complete. There was no longer any question that a book was in the making.

A first draft of this volume was completed by February 1975, and a limited number of copies were mailed out for comments and criticisms. Because the manuscript leaned so heavily on the Blocks' research, their view of how I handled their work was of obvious importance to me. I was also particularly eager to have Susan Coates' reaction, because her research occupied a prominent place in the volume. As Jerome Kagan and I had worked together on an earlier review (in *Carmichael's manual of child psychology*), I also solicited his views. The overall opinion of the first draft was uniformly positive but accompanied by a number of suggestions for improvement. In addition, Susan Coates supplied me with some additional unpublished data that helped to clarify some of the ambiguities in the field-independence domain. She also directed my attention to relevant work that I had overlooked.

As these suggestions arrived in the spring of 1975, other relevant articles were appearing in the journals of developmental psychology, and the program of the Biennial Meeting of the Society for Research in Child Development (Denver, April 1975) included relevant symposia and individual papers. With the arrival of summer 1975, I returned to Maine with the intent of incorporating most of the readers' suggestions as well as the new published and unpublished material into a revised and expanded final draft. I returned to New York City in September determined not to make further changes, but I could not resist the lure of the September 1975 journals. Hence, the volume is as current as the exigencies of time have permitted.

Because earlier reviews of cognitive-style research could be accommodated in the space of single chapters of varying length, a legitimate and nagging question concerned the need for a book-length treatment of cognitive styles in the infancy and early childhood period. Several reasons can be advanced. First and foremost is the heavy reliance on unpublished materials. When it is not possible to cite a reference carrying a full description of a study, more extended treatment is essential if the reader is to comprehend its rationale and outcomes. It can be argued, of course, that it is premature to report findings that have not as yet made their way into print. This matter has troubled me greatly, for it bears on the issue of when knowledge can be considered "official." If written documentation is the *sine qua non*, then this volume can be said to contain much "unofficial" knowledge. I opted for inclusion rather than exclusion of such information because, first, I had great faith in the scientific reputation of the investigators who produced it and, second, I did not believe it would be fair to the reader to omit information at my disposal. I should note that the investigators concerned have read and approved of my treatment of their unpublished data. This volume tries to convey all that we presently know about cognitive styles in the first five years of life. It seemed wiser to report everything, and let the corrective nature of the scientific endeavor weed out "error," rather than try to make dubious distinctions between "official" and "unofficial" knowledge.

Another reason for the book-length treatment of the present topic has to do with the new issues that are raised when cognitive styles are projected into the early childhood period. Without exception, cognitive-style research has emphasized individual differences, whether in adults or children. Developmental concerns have been secondary and have been focused largely on the issue of mean age differences and interindividual stability over time. When the developmental trajectory is extended virtually to infancy, however, a range of new issues is pushed into the foreground. For example, we must ask at what age a style genuinely begins. Are there infant precursors? Is the development of cognitive styles in any way influenced by the stage transitions described by Piaget and other cognitive developmentalists?

Investigators frequently work on common problems but fail to communicate with one another because they operate within different conceptual frameworks. I have tried in the pages of this volume to achieve some articulations. Within the cognitive-style domain, categorizing and conceptualizing styles have occupied a prominent place. In the course of extending these styles into early childhood, one necessarily confronts a major controversial issue among contemporary cognitive developmentalists—the process by which the child forms his earliest concepts and words. Linking the current work in conceptual and semantic development to the older work on categorizing and conceptualizing styles is not readily accomplished. Nonetheless, I have tried to forge as many bridges as possible. The extent to which I have been successful is up to the reader to decide.

It is no exaggeration to state that this volume could not have been written without the contribution of numerous colleagues. Michael Lewis clearly deserves first mention. Without his invitation to prepare a chapter for his recent edited volume, it is certain that this book would never have been conceptualized, let alone written. I am enormously grateful to Jack and Jeanne Block of the University of California at Berkeley for permitting me to rummage through their unpublished data on a one-week visit to their project and for graciously supplying me with additional indispensable material thereafter via the mails. The frequent reference to their work throughout the pages of this volume is, in my opinion, a reflection of its importance for the study of cognitive styles in childhood. I also am indebted to Susan Coates of the Downstate Medical Center, State University of New York, for sending me useful papers and data prior to their publication. I should like to thank Keith Nelson, my colleague in this department, who devoted considerable time to explaining some highly relevant unpublished findings. William Ward, my erstwhile colleague at ETS, provided me with reports of the ETS Head Start Longitudinal Study, his own as well as those of others, and I should like to thank him for it. The various figures contained in the book were reproduced with the kind permission of Susan Coates, Katherine Nelson, Keith Nelson, Henry Ricciuti, Irving Sigel, and John Wright. I would like to thank Kathleen Connor for her invaluable assistance in the preparation of the bibliography. Finally, I owe a special debt of gratitude to Barbara Gombach for tolerating all of the demands placed on her in the course of typing the preliminary and final drafts of the manuscript.

Any book, of course, is a product of both proximal and distal influences. In the latter category are all of those individuals who initially encouraged and subsequently facilitated my research on cognitive processes. It was Jerome Bruner who first pointed the way during my predoctoral and early postdoctoral years at Harvard. I owe him a very special debt. It was Michael Wallach, my former collaborator, who sharpened my thinking about cognition in the course of our joint research and writing during the 1960s. Finally, it was Samuel Messick who during my years at ETS provided the kind of hospitable intellectual climate in which my research and thinking could develop and prosper.

NATHAN KOGAN
New York City

To LAURA

1

Introduction

A. GENERAL BACKGROUND

The construct of cognitive style has been with us for approximately a quarter of a century, and it continues to preoccupy psychologists working in the interface between cognition and personality. There are individual differences in styles of perceiving, remembering, thinking, and judging, and these individual variations, if not directly part of the personality, are at the very least intimately associated with various noncognitive dimensions of personality. It has also been demonstrated that cognitive styles can have an impact on intellectual and academic achievements, a practical aspect that has unquestionably contributed to the massive volume of cognitive-style researches now in print.

With the progressive increase in the output of publications in the domain of cognitive styles, the need for a conceptual integration of the vast body of relevant empirical research has grown commensurably. I, as well as others, have attempted such an integration from a number of different perspectives. Vernon (1973) traces the historical roots of cognitive styles in early twentieth century German typological theories and then critically analyzes contemporary approaches. Bieri (1971) and Kagan and Kogan (1970) consider the diverse theoretical orientations that have distinguished the cognitive-style domain. The latter authors, in addition, focus heavily on developmental aspects, particularly on individual differences in the cognitive functioning of school-age children. Kogan (1971) offers a review of research on cognitive styles from the point of view of their implications for intellectual functioning and academic achievement. Finally, an examination of cognitive styles from a life-span perspective is contained in Kogan (1973). The last essay was primarily concerned with changes in cognitive functioning in middle and old age, because that period of life had been essentially neglected in earlier reviews.

It can readily be seen that the published critical surveys of research on cognitive styles has had little to say about infancy and the preschool period of early childhood. There are rather obvious reasons for this neglect. In respect to infancy, it is simply not possible to obtain meaningful measurements using the currently available operational indices of cognitive styles. These indices, after all, were developed for use with subjects who could respond to verbal instructions. As the infant gradually matures into the preschooler, he or she naturally becomes capable of responding to verbally presented tasks. Even where tasks demand a nonverbal response from the child, some verbal capacity is nevertheless required if the child is to comprehend task instructions. Hence, the limitations on the study of cognitive styles in infancy are not present in the case of the preschooler (in the approximate age range of 2½–5 years), and it is hardly surprising that several relevant research projects devoted to the study of that age group are currently in progress. Some of this work has been published, some is in the form of preprints and unpublished project reports, and some has not yet advanced beyond the stage of computer output. It is the comparatively recent vintage of the relevant work that accounts for its absence from the integrative and critical summaries and analyses of cognitive-style research that have been published within the last 5 years.

This volume, then, represents an effort to acquaint interested readers with some of the more important findings emerging from contemporary research on cognitive styles in preschool children. Because so much of the work is "in progress," so to speak, this work necessarily has a tentative quality. The field, as it presently stands, has not yet arrived at the point where any definitive integration is possible. I should also like to have it known that I have not been personally involved in the research to be described. This is a liability, to be sure, but something can also be said in support of a review undertaken by a dispassionate outsider. It is my hope that my close familiarity and identification with the cognitive-style area through prior research and theoretical analysis can in part compensate for my lack of direct research involvement with the age group under scrutiny in this volume. Earlier, reference was made to my previous publication (Kogan, 1973) devoted to the cognitive styles from a life-span perspective. Regrettably, the earliest years of life could not be encompassed in that review, and, in that sense, the essay failed to do complete justice to the life-span conception. This monograph, then necessarily has a gap-filling quality, as it tries to evaluate the significance of cognitive styles for the early stages of childhood. Until that is accomplished, one cannot really claim that a genuine life-span orientation has been brought to bear on the cognitive style domain.

B.   COGNITIVE STYLES AND INFANCY

Let us return for the moment to the relevance of cognitive styles during infancy. To do justice to this topic, one must introduce the distinction between isomorphic and metamorphic continuities (Bell, Weller, & Waldrop, 1971). Kagan (1971) employs the terms "homotypic" and "heterotypic," respectively, to describe the same distinction. Isomorphic or homotypic continuity carries the implication of stability in the same response modality. Metamorphic or hetero-typic continuity implies stability over time across response classes that are dissimilar but possibly linked together on some theoretical basis. As Lewis (1967) has noted, the latter type of continuity is most typical across the infancy and early childhood years. Lewis, in fact, cites numerous examples of isomorphic instability resulting from changes in the functional meaning of a response over time. A cry, for example, often has quite different significance at 3 and at 12 months of age.

As indicated earlier, links between cognitive styles in early childhood and infant behaviors cannot assume an isomorphic form, given the manner in which cognitive styles have been traditionally operationalized. There may well be metamorphic-heterotypic continuities, however, between certain classes of infant response and subsequent selected indicators of cognitive style in the pre-school years and beyond. It is in that sense that one can speak of precursors of cognitive styles in infancy. Regrettably, it is not possible to say very much about such precursors here, given the general dearth of longitudinal research seeking links between individual variation in infant cognition and cognitive styles in childhood. At the present, it appears that the vast majority of infant research-ers have not been especially interested in predicting childhood variation in cog-nitive style, whereas those studying dimensions of cognitive style in early child-hood have not concerned themselves with infant precursors.[1] The research of Kagan (1971) and his colleagues presently stands as one of the very few attempts to find linkages between behaviors in infancy and cognitive-style indicators in early childhood. Unfortunately, that research appears to have term-inated with an assessment at 27 months of age, an age where the validities of the cognitive-style measurements are somewhat suspect. It should further be noted that the research by Kagan and his colleagues has been concerned exclusively with precursors of a single cognitive style, reflection-impulsivity. More recently, Wilson and Lewis (1974) have searched for precursors at 13 and 25 months of reflection-impulsivity assessed at 44 months of age. Both of the foregoing studies are discussed in Chapter III of this volume.[2]

C. COGNITIVE STYLES IN PRESCHOOL CHILDREN

Given the limited scope of the research on infants, the bulk of this monograph is necessarily devoted to description and discussion of research based on

[1]This dearth of relevant research stands in striking contrast to the vast amount of work that has been devoted to infant precursors of childhood IQ (see Bayley, 1970; McCall, Hogarty, & Hurlburt, 1972).

[2]Cross-cultural investigators (see Munroe & Munroe, 1975) have begun to examine infant care variables in relation to cognitive styles later in childhood.

preschool children. Some of this research is longitudinal in character, permitting an examination of stability and change of cognitive styles during the preschool period. At first blush, one might expect that the isomorphic versus metamorphic or homotypic versus heterotypic distinction would cease to be of relevance beyond the infancy period. One must bear in mind, however, that the tasks developed to assess cognitive styles in adults and older children must generally be modified for administration to young children. Although such modification is inevitable if research is to proceed, an altered task may in some cases portend an altered construct and a consequent reduction in isomorphic-homotypic stability.

It is also feasible, quite apart from effects of task modification, that cognitive differentiation and organization change with age, with the consequence that particular cognitive styles shift their location in the network of dimensional relationships under study. Emmerich (1964, 1968) has discussed this issue in regard to personality development. The implication of such structural change is that one must be prepared to search for heterotypic as well as homotypic stabilities throughout the life span.

Let us pause at this juncture to inquire about the general rationale for the study of cognitive styles in preschool children. Some investigators are clearly interested in the preschool period as such, and cognitive styles offer a means of exploring the cognitive diversity of young children in a way that is not feasible with a monolithic IQ index. Furthermore, the general theoretical richness of the cognitive-style domain far exceeds that of the global intelligence construct. Indeed, the fact that cognitive styles share variance with both personality and intelligence indices can serve to shed light on the mechanisms responsible for relationships reported to exist between those domains. The general aim of the foregoing approach, then, is to achieve an understanding of cognition-personality dynamics in the preschool child. The introduction of such "extrinsic" variables as sex, social class, and parental child-rearing practices are not incompatible with the approach outlined.

Other investigators, with a more strictly developmental perspective, study the preschool child in the hope of tracking the origins of cognitive styles. It may be stretching a point, but it is not unlikely that these investigators nourish the hope of extending the homotypic continuities of adulthood, adolescence, and later childhood down to the preschool level. If this goal should be reached (that is, if the psychological meaning of cognitive styles remains constant from the preschool years through the remainder of the life span), the developmental analysis of cognitive styles would assume an elegant coherence and simplicity. Such an achievement, in fact, would almost certainly lend renewed vigor to the search for infant precursors. The major point to be stressed is that the focus is not on the preschool child as such, but on the delineation of the continuities and discontinuities with adjacent and more distant segments of the life span.

No doubt, the distinction between the two approaches outlined above has been somewhat exaggerated for rhetorical purposes. The same investigator can naturally be interested both in the role of cognitive styles in the psychology of the preschool child and in the continuity or discontinuity of cognitive styles across the preschool period and the years that follow. As the relevant research comes under review, however, the emphasis on one or the other orientation should become manifest.

D. TYPES OF COGNITIVE STYLES

So far, we have spoken of cognitive styles in general and global terms, without distinguishing among the diverse kinds of cognitive styles that have been subjected to empirical study. Messick (1970) defines nine cognitive styles, and it is quite likely that the list can be expanded by adding other dimensions of individual variation in cognitive functioning that are stylistic in nature. As may be expected, the various styles currently extant differ from one another in numerous respects. The diverse theoretical backgrounds of the various cognitive styles is discussed elsewhere (Kagan & Kogan, 1970; Vernon, 1973) and so need not concern us here. The styles also differ markedly in the sheer level of empirical attention that has been directed toward them. At the one extreme, hundreds, if not thousands, of articles pertaining to the field independence-dependence construct have been published since the appearance of *Personality through perception* (Witkin, Lewis, Hertzman, Machover, Meissner, & Wapner, 1954). At the opposite extreme, the construct of "tolerance for unrealistic experiences" has generated only a loose handful of studies since the Klein and Schlesinger (1951) publication introduced that particular cognitive style to the psychological community.

There are other, possibly more fruitful, ways in which cognitive styles can be classified. Kogan (1973) offers a threefold classification based on the distance of the style in question from the domain of abilities. Type I is closest to the ability domain, for performance on the operational index of the style can be described as more or less veridical. For example, the individual described as field independent is more proficient in setting the rod to the vertical in the rod-and-frame test than is the field-dependent person. Because the task requirement is to set the rod at the true vertical, field independence necessarily implies a superior level of performance.[3]

In Type II cognitive styles, the question of veridicality of performance does not arise. Nevertheless, the investigator places greater value on one specific kind of performance relative to another. Typical are the conceptualization styles

[3]Wachtel (1972a) maintains, in fact, that the use of the term "style" to characterize such performance is unjustified. Instead he believes that any measures having better or worse implications reflect "the degree to which an individual possesses the basic tools and attributes upon which particular styles and strategies must rest [p. 782]." In short, the Type I category, in Wachtel's terms, necessarily refers to prerequisites for particular styles and strategies, not to styles and strategies as such.

described by Kagan, Moss, and Sigel (1963). Although an analytic style in no sense represents a higher level of veridicality than a thematic-relational style, the investigators place greater value on the former. Such a value choice is some-times made on purely theoretical grounds—one style is postulated to be "devel-opmentally more advanced" than another. The value aspect may also derive from observed empirical correlates of the styles in question. If one style cor-relates significantly with ability indexes, whereas an alternative style does not, the former tends to be endowed with greater value.

Consider, finally, styles belonging to Type III. In this case, considerations of veridicality are again irrelevant, and differential value is not assigned to one or the other pole of the stylistic dimension. For example, a broad versus narrow style of categorization (e.g., Pettigrew, 1958) was initially advanced in largely value-neutral terms. Since that time, investigators have not found a consistent pattern of correlates to suggest that either broad or narrow categorizers have a consistent cognitive advantage (Kogan, 1971). Hence, categorization style has remained basically value neutral, but this does not rule out the possibility of future research outcomes forcing a Type III cognitive style to be reclassified as Type II.

Let us consider some developmental implications of the foregoing classification. Where cognitive styles of Type I are concerned, we are operating in a domain with clear capacity-like properties. The child requested to find the simple figure embedded in a complex design (one of the major indexes of field independence-dependence) is either capable or not capable of performing the task. Much as any test of ability or intelligence administered to preschool children, tests of field independence, such as the Embedded Figures Test (EFT), can be scaled down to a level of difficulty appropriate for this young age group. Because correlates of EFT performance have been quite thoroughly examined in older children (Witkin, Dyk, Faterson, Goodenough, & Karp, 1962), one can readily determine whether the same general pattern of correlates emerges at the preschool level. Evidence for similarity in correlational patterns would strengthen the claim of continuity of the field-independence construct into the preschool years. We shall in due course consider research directly focused on this issue.

Cognitive styles designated as Types II and III raise other kinds of issues. In adults and adolescents, tasks that tap categorizing and conceptualizing styles often involve a strategic choice or preference on the part of the subject. The individual generally recognizes that more than a single response option is available and hence is likely to choose the one that appears to offer the most elegant, appropriate, or satisfying solution. For example, in the task requiring the sorting or grouping of common objects, we can expect that most adults recognize diverse grouping options, but choose those that meet some subjective standard of acceptability. As the sample under study decreases in age, there is good reason to believe that the response options narrow. Where preschool

children constitute the sample under study, it is quite possible that a substantial number are not capable of more than a single mode of response. In
other words, tasks that assess stylistic preferences at older ages may well be
tapping capacities at younger ages. If there is any truth to the foregoing generalization, one may expect to find Type II and III cognitive styles correlating
more highly with abilities in preschool samples than in samples of older
individuals.

E. CRITERIA FOR SELECTION OF PARTICULAR COGNITIVE STYLES

An obvious rationale exists for the choice of particular cognitive styles to
include in this monograph. The fundamental criterion for inclusion is the availability of a body of evidence on preschool children relevant to the style in
question. When this criterion is applied, five of the nine cognitive styles listed
by Messick (1970) fall by the wayside. Four of these five—scanning, leveling vs
sharpening, constricted vs flexible control, and tolerance for incongruous or
unrealistic experiences—derive from the program of research initiated by Klein
and Gardner and their associates at the Menninger Foundation (e.g., Gardner,
Holzman, Klein, Linton, & Spence, 1959). The major portion of their research
is based on adults. Gardner and Moriarty (1968) have studied the four cognitive styles at issue in a sample of 9- to 13-year-old children, which appears to
represent the youngest age group examined by Gardner and his colleagues.
Other investigators, however, have extended the research to children as young
as 6 years of age (e.g., Santostefano, 1964; Santostefano & Paley, 1964).

It is important to note that the program of research conducted by Gardner
and his colleagues at the Menninger Foundation (and subsequently by Klein,
Spence, and their colleagues and students at New York University) has derived
from an ego-psychoanalytic tradition (e.g., Hartmann, 1968). A number of
prominent infancy researchers (e.g., Escalona, 1968; Korner, 1964; Murphy,
1962) are closely identified with that particular tradition, yet no effort has
been made to articulate the infancy work with the emergence of cognitive
styles in the preschool period. Korner (1964) has speculated on the possible
nature of such links. In her auditory stimulation experiments, some infants
responded with a large repertoire of reactions, whereas other infants manifested
a more singular and global responsiveness. The latter is described as a possible
sensorimotor antecedent to the cognitive style of leveling (that is, a tendency
to blur distinctions between memory images and current perceptions). Of
course, we are treated here to a promissory note of a highly speculative character. It is presented merely to indicate that a desire has been expressed in
ego-psychoanalytic quarters to achieve some articulation between infant
behaviors and subsequent ego structures (within which cognitive styles are

presumed to occupy an important place). To the best of my knowledge, however, the possibilities of articulation have not yet been realized.

Consider next the fifth cognitive style that receives limited consideration in this volume. This style is labeled cognitive complexity vs simplicity and concerns the number of dimensions that individuals employ in construing their social and personal worlds. As developed by Bieri (1961), the style under discussion reflects differentiation exclusively, that is, the number of different dimensions or constructs available to the individual. Subsequently, Bieri (1966) has proposed that consideration also be given to the "articulation" of one's constructs (that is, whether essentially dichotomous or more finely graded). An alternative conceptualization (Harvey, Hunt, & Schroder, 1961) attempts to broaden the cognitive complexity construct to include the hierarchical organization of an individual's constructs or dimensions.

Kagan and Kogan (1970) and Kogan (1971) offer a review and critique of developmentally oriented research inspired by both of the approaches described above. As in the case of the research inspired by ego psychology, there are numerous studies based on adult and adolescent samples, a few studies on older children, and nothing where preschool children are concerned. This lack of relevant work exists in spite of the strong developmental flavor of the Harvey, Hunt, and Schroder (1961) conceptualization and in spite of Bieri's (1966) urging that developmentally oriented research can proceed if investigators focus on the components of the style (for example, the number and variety of dimensions and the articulation of those dimensions). Signell (1966) reported a study directed precisely to Bieri's point, but the youngest children studied were 9 years old. It seems dubious that the construct of cognitive complexity is too complex to be studied in younger children. More likely, workers in the cognitive complexity domain have not been sufficiently oriented along developmental lines to make the difficult effort of adapting procedures for use with children of preschool age.

There is another tradition of research in the domain of complexity that has so far been studied quite independently of cognitive style. The tradition can be traced to the writings of Berlyne (1960), Hunt (1965), and Fiske and Maddi (1961), among others, and it attempts to deal with the issue of "preference for stimulus complexity." The thrust of the developmental research emanating from this theoretical tradition has been directed toward the effect of variations in stimulus complexity on exploration, curiosity, and play (e.g., Nunnally & Lemond, 1973; Switzky, Haywood, & Isett, 1974). Age and sex differences in children have also been examined, but within-age individual differences, although quite pronounced, have been of peripheral concern. Conceivably, a young child's level of preference for complexity (as indexed, for example, by choices of play objects independently graded for complexity) represents an antecedent of later cognitive complexity or simplicity. At the present time, evidence relevant to this issue is not available.

This concludes the justification for omitting particular cognitive styles from consideration in the present work. We can now proceed to a discussion of the four cognitive styles comprising the major portion of this monograph. These are field independence-dependence, reflection-impulsivity, styles of categorization (breadth vs narrowness), and styles of conceptualization (analytic, categorical, and functional-thematic). Separate chapters of this volume are devoted to each. These are followed by a chapter concerned with interrelationships among the styles. A final chapter offers a limited integration in the form of a set of conclusions.

For each of the four styles under consideration, a number of fundamental issues are raised. Given the general orientation of this volume, the relationship between each of the styles and intelligence is of foremost importance. If one is willing to accept the presumption that cognitive differentiation increases with age, it is conceivable that a general ability dimension pervades all cognitive assessments in early childhood, implying a high degree of shared variance between styles and capacity. Such an outcome would not be consistent with other evidence (Stott & Ball, 1965) suggesting that the ability domain itself is multidimensional in infants and preschool children. Guilford (1967) and Messick (1973) strongly assert that the evidence does not support the Garrett (1946) hypothesis of a single general ability in early childhood that becomes differentiated over time. On this basis, links between indexes of cognitive style and ability in preschool children should not be particularly strong. Of course, the extent of the relationship necessarily varies with the cognitive style at issue. Type I styles should engage the most ability variance, and Type III the least.

Other aspects of the four cognitive styles that are to engage our attention include age and sex differences over the preschool period, both in mean level and in the pattern of correlations with other variables. Consideration is also given to the observed continuity or discontinuity between the findings obtained at preschool and later ages. Finally, the exceedingly limited evidence regarding infant precursors of cognitive style will claim our attention. Throughout the discussion, every effort has been made to elucidate the cognitive and personality dynamics underlying each of the styles under review. It is assumed, however, that the reader is not confronting cognitive styles for the first time. Exceedingly thorough reviews of the cognitive-style literature have been published (see references cited earlier), and it is my intention to minimize the overlap between this monograph and previously published reviews.

II
Field Independence—Dependence

A. GENERAL BACKGROUND

Of the three indices of field independence-dependence developed by Witkin and his colleagues—the body adjustment test (BAT), the rod-and-frame test (RFT), and the Embedded Figures Test (EFT)—the latter two (largely because of the simplicity of the apparatus and ease of administration) have clearly become the principal procedures for assessing the construct under consideration. This construct has assumed many different labels in addition to field independence-dependence (for example, analytic versus global, field articulation, psychological differentiatioh), but the style basically concerns a capacity to overcome embedding contexts in perception, i.e., to separate a part from an organized whole. The Witkin group has long been interested in the developmental stability of their cognitive style, and they have published a long-term longitudinal study (Witkin, Goodenough, & Karp, 1967) indicating a substantial degree of interindividual consistency in two separate samples (one tested at 8 and 13 years and the other tested at 10, 14, 17, and 24 years of age). Also noted were progressive increases in field independence over the age span indicated. These outcomes represent an impressive display of continuity of a cognitive construct over a significant portion of the life span. At the same time, investigation of younger age periods was inhibited given the exceptional difficulty of the original procedures for younger children. Accordingly, a strong impetus existed for the development of procedures appropriate for children younger than 10 years. In due course, Karp and Konstadt (1963) produced a Children's Embedded Figures Test (CEFT) appropriate for children as young as 5 years (see also Witkin, Oltman, Raskin, & Karp, 1971). In contrast to the purely geometric stimuli used in the adult form, the CEFT consists of a series of complex meaningful stimuli in which simple figures are embedded. Also contributing to the study of field independence-dependence in young children was the development of a portable rod-and-frame apparatus (Oltman, 1968) that markedly enhanced the ease of administration of that particular procedure. In the case of both the CEFT and the portable RFT, the sum of the empirical evidence appears to support the view that the field independence-dependence construct has remained intact despite the task modifications required to assess the construct in younger children. As of the present time, it is reasonable to assume that the long-term stability of field independence-dependence can, at the very least, be extended downward to the first year of school.

After approximately 25 years of research on the construct of field independence-dependence, it is hardly surprising that the Witkin group, as well as many other investigators, has related that construct to a wide variety of other variables. Some of the latter have assumed the status of "favorites," and we have now reached the point where it is not always possible to distinguish between criterial measures of the construct as such and important correlates of the construct. Witkin et al. (1962) have tried to deal with this problem by broadening their construct to include a variety of psychological dimensions presumed to be indicative of "psychological differentiation." The difficulty with this kind of broadening and relabeling is that the expanded construct often fails to accommodate other forms of psychological functioning that have as much "right" to be included within a "differentiation" rubric as do the favored variables.

The arguments for and against the construct of "psychological differentiation" as employed by Witkin and his colleagues have been elaborated elsewhere (e.g., Kagan & Kogan, 1970; Wachtel, 1972b) and so need not concern us further here. Let us for the moment accept the idea of the broader construct and consider the one index—articulation of the body concept (ABC)—for which data on preschool children presently exists. Although ABC has no obvious connection with disembedding capacity in perception, there is little doubt that the former is often employed as an alternative index of field independence-dependence (e.g., Corah, 1965; Faterson & Witkin, 1970). ABC is assessed with a figure-drawing test in which subjects are asked to produce figures of their own and the opposite sex in that order. These drawings are then scored on a five-point articulation scale, the highest score going to sophisticated, detailed drawings with high form level and the lowest score assigned to primitive drawings with low form level. [1]

Faterson and Witkin (1970) discuss two longitudinal studies based on the 8-13 and 10-24 year age groups described by Witkin et al. (1967). The ABC results essentially parallel those reported earlier for the EFT and RFT; that is, ABC scores increased with age (but leveled off after age 14) and long-term sta-

---

[1] It should be noted that the validity issue—whether high ABC scores actually reflect high articulation of subjects' own bodies or are simply an indication of superior drawing ability—has not been adequately resolved.

bility obtained over the age span under examination. Consistent with these findings, those subjects designated as more field independent at each age on the basis of an EFT-RFT composite also achieved higher scores on the ABC scale. The one exception to the pattern of evidence reported previously for EFT and RFT was the reversal in the direction of the sex difference. Females achieved higher scores than did males on the ABC index, a finding that Faterson and Witkin (1970) consider an artifact of the elaboration of clothing and adornments in the drawings of the female figure by female subjects. On the whole, the longitudinal evidence for ABC in no way alters the pattern of coherence, consistency, and long-term stability that characterizes the field-independence construct from the early school years through adulthood. Let us now see whether the construct remains intact in children of preschool age.

B.   ASSESSMENT IN PRESCHOOL CHILDREN

1.   Measures of Field Independence-Dependence

Can field independence-dependence be reliably assessed in children of preschool age? Coates (1972) has developed a Preschool Embedded Figures Test (PEFT) specifically intended for children in the age range of 3-5 years. The instrument is rather similar to the CEFT (indeed, nine of the 27 complex stimulus figures were directly taken from the CEFT), but the overall task was simplified by the removal of color and the reduction of the number of distracting simple forms in the complex figure. For each of the items, the child is required to locate a simple equilateral triangle embedded in the figure by tracing it with his finger. An illustrative item from the PEFT is shown in Fig. 1. Another version of the EFT suitable for preschool children has been developed by Banta (1970), the Early Childhood Embedded Figures Test (EC-EFT). The latter is highly similar to the PEFT but has not been the target of as extensive a standardization and research effort. Internal-consistency reliabilities for two samples in Banta's research were .48 and .59. For six samples described in Coates (1972), these coefficients ranged from .74 to .91. Equally high PEFT reliabilities are reported by Block and Block (1973) and by Dermen and Meissner (1972). These data are clearly in support of the psychometric superiority of the PEFT.

In Witkin's operational formulation of the field-independent versus field-dependent cognitive styles, the RFT is given equal weight with the EFT in a composite index (e.g., Witkin *et al.*, 1962) on the basis of the substantial correlation found between these two measures. Results reported by Dreyer, Dreyer, and Nebelkopf (1971), who used the CEFT and the portable RFT, suggest that the strong relationship can be extended down to kindergarten children ranging in age from 5 to 6 years (rs of $-.61$ and $-.66$ for 162 boys

FIG. 1   Sample item from the Coates Preschool Embedded Figures Test, with simple figure shown at upper right. (Reprinted with permission of Consulting Psychologist Press, Inc.)

and 138 girls, respectively). For children 4-5 years of age, however, the PEFT-RFT relationship appears to break down. Block and Block[2] report nonsignificant correlations of $-.22$ and $.07$ in boys and girls, respectively. Similar findings are reported by Coates (personal communication, 1975) in an unpublished study based on two samples of middle-class 4- to-5-year-old boys and girls (Ns ranging from 22 to 29). For boys, rs of $.01$ and $.29$ were obtained; for girls, the comparable rs were $-.07$ and $.27$. None of these rs approached statistical significance. In one of the samples, Coates tried to make the task more interesting for the children by placing a facade of a house over the RFT and substituting a tall slender doll for the rod. This did not alter the PEFT-RFT relationship to any appreciable extent (nonsignificant rs of $.26$ and $.23$ for boys and girls, respectively). It should be further noted that these correlations are generally in a direction opposite to the predicted relation, for large RFT scores reflect greater deviation of the rod from the vertical. In a final modification with the same sample, Coates used a rod and frame placed on a wall without any

[2]No date is provided when reference is to unpublished data from the Block and Block (1973) project.

visual obstruction or physical restraint of the child. On a second trial of this task, a large standard (2 × 18 inches) was placed approximately 5 inches to the left of the RFT and the child was asked to make the stick in the middle stand up straight just like the one on the side. With the foregoing modifications, the PEFT-RFT correlations turned statistically significant for the girls (rs of −.41 and −.43 without and with the standard, respectively). The corresponding rs in boys (−.12 and −.11), in contrast, were emphatically nonsignificant.

The foregoing outcomes suggest that it is possible to present the RFT to pre-schoolers in a form that yields performances having something in common with disembedding skill on the PEFT.[3] It must be granted that the expected relation-ship emerged only in the case of girls. Such a sex difference is no cause for dis-tress, however, for it may simply mean that a coherent construct of field inde-pendence-dependence emerges somewhat earlier in females than in males. Con-sistent with this latter inference is the evidence (in both of Coates' samples under consideration) that the articulation of body concept (ABC) index cor-related significantly with PEFT for girls (rs of .59 and .54), but not for boys (rs of .20 and .27). It becomes clear as we proceed with our review that the earlier emergence of a construct for females relative to males is characteristic not only of field independence-dependence but of other cognitive styles as well.

Given the kind of sex difference observed, it is not possible to maintain, of course, that Witkin's construct remains completely intact into the preschool years. For boys younger than 5 years of age, the PEFT, RFT, and ABC do not seem to comprise a coherent cluster of measures. Even in girls, as we have just noted, the portable form of the RFT devised by Oltman does not seem to tap the sort of skill reflected in older children's performance.[4] It is hardly sur-prising, then, to note the absence of significant relationships between the por-table RFT and perceptual-analytic abilities in Block and Block's 4-year-old sample (in contrast with the positive findings for the PEFT). Such evidence for differential validity cannot be considered definitive, however, given the method variance that the perceptual-analytic ability tests share with the PEFT, but not with the RFT. A crucial validity comparison must necessarily concern predicted correlates of PEFT and RFT that do not share method variance with either.

---

[3]In a personal communication (1974), Jeanne Block comments on the difficulty of restraining a 4 year old from wiggling and removing his head from the chin rest in the portable RFT apparatus. It is therefore of special significance that a PEFT-RFT relationship has emerged for the Coates variation of the RFT that eliminates such physical restraints.

[4]A personal communication (1975) from Susan Coates reports that preschool children are bored by the RFT, and hence considerable effort is required to keep their attention focused on the task. Coates also asserts that the PEFT, in marked contrast to the RFT, appears to be inherently interesting for most preschool children. These observations, along with those of Block (see Footnote 3), suggest that there may be more error variance in RFT measurement at the preschool level than is the case for PEFT and ABC indexes.

Furthermore, it is now quite clear that the Coates variation of the RFT should be employed (at least for girls) if there is to be a fair comparison. Given the exceedingly limited data available for that method, it is apparent that the validational burden must be borne by the more extensively studied PEFT.

2.   Developmental Mean Differences

Consider next the issue of mean differences in level of field independence across the preschool years. In the case of Oltman's (1968) portable RFT, cross-sectional data based on 100 male and 100 female children across the age range of 4 to 13 years yielded a significant linear increase in field independence with age for both sexes (Vaught, Pittman, & Roodin, 1975). Within the preschool period in that study, males manifested a massive increase in field independence between the ages of 5 and 6 years, whereas an increase of comparable magnitude in females occurred between the ages of 4 and 5 years. Coates (1972) reports a significant progressive increase across the age span of 3-5 years in level of dis-embedding skill on the PEFT for both boys and girls. A similar increase was observed for children ranging from 42 to 65 months of age in the ETS Head Start longitudinal study (Dermen & Meissner, 1972). Coates (1972) also refers to unpublished data by Waldrop for children approximately 33 months of age in which mean levels are markedly lower than for Coates' 3-year-olds. It appears that the PEFT has not been administered to children younger than 33 months of age. Because Waldrop's subjects responded successfully to one-third of the PEFT items on the average, it is conceivable that the PEFT could be administered to children even younger in age without a marked reduction in inter-individual variance. In support of this supposition is the indication in Kagan's (1971) research that an embedded figures test can be administered to children as young as 27 months of age. In the Kagan version of the EFT, three simple figures in the form of black and white line drawings—a cat, a car, and a flower—were embedded in backgrounds that varied in complexity.

Where the articulation of body-concept (ABC) measure is concerned, Ford, Stern, and Dillon (1974) have reported data on draw-a-person task performance based on 58 children between 36 and 72 months of age. Highly significant age differences in the anticipated direction were observed.

3.   Stability of Assessments

Is field independence-dependence, when assessed in the preschool years, tapping essentially the same construct as assessed in later childhood and adulthood? An affirmative answer to the question would obviously permit a downward age extension of the field independence-dependence construct and virtually establish its continuity over that large portion of the life span where testing with verbally administered instructions is feasible. Although findings consistent with a continuity position have been reported, other evidence is available that is not entirely congruent with such a stance.

The most relevant and direct type of evidence in regard to the continuity question would necessarily derive from longitudinal research spanning the preschool and subsequent years of childhood. Although studies of this type are in progress (e.g., Block & Block, 1973; Shipman, 1972), analysis of relationships between preschool and school-age measures is in its incipient stages and not yet available for inclusion in this volume. Hence, we are forced to rely on inferences derived from the pattern of correlations obtained at different age levels. In this respect, it is just as important to investigate the similarity of the pattern within the preschool period as between the latter and later periods of childhood.

Coates (1972) reports test-retest correlations over a 5-month interval ranging from .69 to .75 in three small samples of 3 and 4 year-old boys and girls. As the time interval between testing increased, the coefficients of stability, as expected, declined. In the ETS longitudinal study of 750 3- to 5-year-old Head Start children (Derman & Meissner, 1972), a stability coefficient of .39 is reported over an approximate 9-month interval. Block and Block examined the stability of PEFT scores over a 1-year period (ages 3-4 years) and obtained coefficients of .49 for 38 boys and .54 for 42 girls. Those authors also obtained the stability of disembedding skill for children first assessed at age 4 years with the PEFT and subsequently assessed at age 5 years with the CEFT. For boys, stability remained significant ($r = .43$, $N = 43$); for girls, in contrast, stability diminished to a nonsignificant level ($r = .14$, $N = 43$). This sex difference in homotypic continuity does not lend itself to any apparent explanation. It is a source of concern, however, for the CEFT represents the transition instrument between the PEFT and the adult EFT. Before the conclusion that boys and girls genuinely differ in stability of field independence-dependence is accepted, however, replication of the Block and Block finding in other samples is clearly required.

C. VALIDATION AT THE PRESCHOOL LEVEL

1. Relation to Intelligence Assessments

Equal in importance to the issues of stability and coherence is the discriminant validity of field-independence indices during the preschool years. Are these validities comparable to those obtained at later ages? In dealing with this issue, Coates (1972, 1975) and Coates and Bromberg (1973) have focused on the relationship between the PEFT and the subtests of the WPPSI (Wechsler, 1967). When factor analysis was applied to the test data of preschoolers, the PEFT was found to load a perceptual-analytic factor (Block Design and Geometric Design) and not to load a verbal-comprehension factor (Information, Vocabulary, Similarities, Comprehension, Sentences). These outcomes bear a strong resemblance to those obtained in the case of the WISC (Wechsler, 1949) and the CEFT by Goodenough and Karp (1961). At the same time, it must be noted that the PEFT was significantly correlated with WPPSI Vocabulary in 4-year-old boys, although not in girls.

In the case of the ETS Head Start sample, Dermen and Meissner (1972) found significant correlations (in the low 30s) between PEFT and such verbally oriented intelligence measures as the Preschool Inventory (Cooperative Tests and Services, 1970) and the Peabody Picture Vocabulary Test (PPVT) (Dunn, 1965). Regrettably, these outcomes represent combined samples of boys and girls, hence precluding comparison with the sex difference reported by Coates. To add a further discordant note, Block and Block found no significant relation in either sex between PEFT and verbal intelligence measures—the PPVT for 3-year-olds and the WPPSI Vocabulary for 4-year-olds. This striking difference in correlational pattern between the ETS Head Start and the Block and Block projects may possibly reflect the wider distribution of scores (particularly at the low end) in a Head Start as opposed to a university nursery-school sample. On the side of convergent validity, however, both of the foregoing projects reported significant correlations between PEFT and other perceptual-analytic cognitive tests, although Block and Block did not find identical correlates for boys and girls (for example, rs of .40 and .22, respectively, with Ravens Progressive Matrices).

2. Relation to Socioemotional and Task-Oriented Behavior

Coates (1972) describes a study in which 56 4-year-old children (28 of each sex) were rated on a series of Q sort items (Schachter, Cooper, & Gordet, 1968) by two nursery-school teachers who had taught the children for an entire year. "Autonomous achievement striving" items (for example, "has urge for independence," "is goal directed in activities," "initiates activities," "avid to learn new things") correlated positively and significantly with PEFT in boys and girls. Other items (for example, "requires structure and direction," "gives up in face of frustration") correlated negatively and significantly with PEFT in both sexes. When WPPSI vocabulary scores were held constant, however, the great majority of the resultant partial correlations remained statistically significant only in the case of the girls. It will be recalled that a field-independence cluster had emerged in Coates' data for girls (but not for boys) between 4 and 5 years of age. Hence, the validation against "real-world" task behaviors, although only partially successful, is highly consistent with other evidence bearing on preschool sex differences.

A replication of the foregoing study has been carried out by Coates and Lord (unpublished data, 1973) on a sample of middle-class children between 4 and 5 years of age (29 girls and 24 boys). A comparison of these data with those reported in Coates (1972) indicates a high degree of agreement. For the girls, all nine of the Q items assigned to the "autonomous achievement striving" cluster in the earlier work continued to be significantly associated with PEFT scores (with verbal ability held constant) in the replication study. Whereas only one of the nine Q items for the boys survived the partial correlational analysis (WPPSI Vocabulary controlled) in the original Coates (1972) study, six of the nine were related significantly to the PEFT in the anticipated direction in the Coates and Lord replication. In all six instances, however, the correlation coefficients were substantially higher for the girls than the boys—median rs (ignoring sign) of .63 and .43, respectively. Once again, then, we observe how the girls (for whom field-independence measures clustered together) yielded higher levels of behavioral validity, although it must be granted that the replication data materially strengthen the case for the behavioral validity of the PEFT in both girls and boys.

The Block and Block project has also utilized Q sort methodology, thus offering the possibility of comparison with the Q sort results reported by Coates. Again, children were independently rated by two or three nursery-school teachers whose acquaintance with the children extended over several months. Separate analyses were undertaken at ages 3 and 4 years. The general drift of the findings indicated a considerable lack of consistency across both age and sex. The PEFT-Q item correlations were distinctly more modest than those reported by Coates, and the evidence for a highly discriminating cluster of "autonomous achievement striving" items was rather weak.

In the case of the 3-year-olds, high-PEFT boys were rated as having high standards of performance for self, high intellectual capacity and high verbal fluency, and an active fantasy life but as avoiding nonverbal methods of communication. At the .10 level of significance, high-PEFT boys were rated as resourceful in initiating activities, not restless and fidgety, having unusual thought processes, attentive and able to concentrate, talkative, competent, skillful, and creative. This latter cluster of behaviors approximates some of the items on the Coates list, but more puzzling was the failure of certain highly relevant items in the California Child Q sort to yield significant discriminations given their manifest relation to autonomous achievement striving (for example, is self-relient, confident; is curious and exploring, eager for new experiences; is persistent, does not give up easily; becomes strongly involved in what he does; seeks to be independent and autonomous).

None of the items just cited turned significant for the 4-year-old boys. Instead, with few exceptions, the same items differentiated high- and low-PEFT boys at 3 and 4 years of age. On the whole, then, the Block and Block Q sort data tend to support the view that high-PEFT boys are more fluent, competent, attentive, and creative than their low-PEFT counterparts. These relationships cannot readily be attributed to verbal aptitude differences between low- and high-PEFT boys, given the exceedingly marginal correlations between PEFT and verbal IQ indices in the Block and Block data. At the same time, the California Child Q sort items most suggestive of "autonomous achievement striving" did not relate to PEFT, hence detracting from Coates' claim that the link between PEFT and "autonomous achievement striving" is as strong in preschoolers as in older children (Crandall & Sinkeldam, 1964).

The Block and Block data for 3- and 4-year-old girls are even less supportive of the foregoing hypothesis. At 3 years of age, high-PEFT girls did not attempt to transfer blame to others, did not express negative feelings directly and openly, and showed a recognition of others' feelings (empathic). These significant relationships between PEFT and Q items disappeared in the 4-year-old girls and were not replaced by any other significant associations (that is, at the .05 level or better). The contrast with the Coates' data is truly striking. Hence, one is forced to the conclusion that an adequate validation of the PEFT based on Q sort evaluations by nursery-school teachers has not yet been satisfactorily accomplished.

Banta (1970) has also tried to validate his version of the Embedded Figures Test (the EC-EFT) against evaluations by nursery-school teachers. A task-competence score was obtained based on ratings of task absorption, persistence, and whether challenged by hard tasks. All are similar to scales included in Coates' "autonomous achievement striving" cluster. The correlation between EC-EFT and task competence in a sample of 80 lower class children was .52. In contrast, the correlation of EC-EFT with social competence was a mere .27. Regrettably, Banta has ignored sex and age differences (children varied in age from 3 to 6 years) and has overlooked the substantial correlation between EC-EFT and Stanford-Binet IQ (r = .37). Once again, then, validation by teacher evaluation is left unsettled.

In Witkin's (1973) more recent writing, one can detect a shift away from a global value bias favoring field independence over field dependence toward a more balanced perspective emphasizing the different virtues represented at each pole of the dimension. It is now maintained that field dependents are strongly oriented toward their social environment and, as a consequence, are distinguished by high levels of social sensitivity and competence. Field independents, in contrast, are presumed to be more task oriented and more focused on the physical environment. Although considerable evidence in favor of the foregoing distinction exists for older children, adolescents, and adults, the issue has only recently been explored at the preschool level. An indirect approach to the problem was contained in a study by Dreyer, McIntire, and Dreyer (1973), who asked 113 kindergarten children to choose classmates with whom they would like to play in a social (free play) situation and with whom they would like to work in a task situation. Sociometric status was computed for both criteria, and their correlation proved to be very high (rs ranging from .84 to .91 across the four subgroups defined by sex and high vs low field dependence). It is therefore evident that the same children tend to be chosen across social and task criteria, suggesting the presence of a general popularity factor. Despite the high correlations just reported, Dreyer et al. (1973) nevertheless attempted to test their major hypothesis that "field-independent children will be chosen more often in a task situation; field-dependent children will be chosen more in a social situation [p. 408]." Field independence-dependence was assessed with a composite of the portable RFT and the CEFT. The foregoing hypothesis received only partial confirmation. Girls with higher sociometric status in the free-play situation were more likely to be field dependent; no such relation was observed in the case of the boys. Sociometric status in the task situation bore no relation whatever to level of field independence-dependence. In stereotypical fashion, boys were more popular than girls on the task criterion.

Dreyer and his associates do not offer an adequate explanation for the failure of the hypothesis to hold in its entirety. Without any doubt, the exceptionally high correlations across the two sociometric criteria raise some concern about kindergarten children's capacity or desire to distinguish between task and social situations when designating liked peers. At the same time, the fact that some such differentiation does occur for the girls in respect to field independence-dependence reinforces Coates' evidence regarding the more salient behavioral correlates of that cognitive style observed in girls relative to boys. It necessarily follows that differential choices of peers along social versus task lines relate to field independence-dependence only if the latter represents a coherent dimension with distinctive behavioral correlates. The evidence so far considered tends to support the view (although hardly unequivocally) that field independence-dependence emerges as a coherent dimension somewhat earlier in girls than boys and, possibly as a consequence, carries along a more salient set of correlates for girls than for boys.

As indicated earlier, the approach of Dreyer and his associates to the issue of social versus task or people versus object orientation is quite indirect. An alternative validational approach of a more direct nature is offered by Coates, Lord, and Jakabovics (1975). The point of departure for their study is the evidence in school-age children that field dependents are more sensitive than field independents to the facial and social cues provided by the examiner in experimental problem-solving situations (Konstadt & Forman, 1965; Ruble & Nakamura, 1972). On this basis, Coates et al. (1975) predicted that preschool children, consistent with their status as field dependent or field independent, respectively, would engage in socially oriented or solitary task activities in the nursery-school setting. Although there is a considerable leap from orienting to the social cues emitted by an adult examiner in an experimental situation to choosing to play with one's peers rather than alone in a nursery-school setting, the sum total of the published evidence based on adults and older children nevertheless clearly points to a stronger orientation toward people and social stimuli in field-dependent individuals, toward things and impersonal tasks in field-independent persons.

In the research of Coates *et al.* (1975), 4- to 5-year-old boys and girls were ranked by their two teachers in order of the amount of time spent in one of five activities over the course of the year: (1) plays with others in the doll corner, (2) plays formal games, (3) plays with others in the block corner, (4) plays alone at the task table, and (5) plays alone with blocks. The first three activities entailed social interaction among the children; the latter two activities were clearly solitary in nature.

Results for boys were highly consistent with theoretical expectations, for field-independent boys were more inclined to "play alone at the task table," whereas field-dependent boys preferred to "play with others in the block corner." Hence, the social-solitary distinction was quite clear-cut in the data for the boys.

The findings for girls were considerably more equivocal. As expected, choosing to "play with others in doll corner" was significantly related to field dependence. Field independence, however, was associated with a preference for playing in the block corner, whether alone or with others. Thus, the social-solitary distinction ceased to be a completely valid one in the case of the girls, and considerations of task content assumed an important role.[5] In this connection, it should be noted that playing in the block corner was significantly more attractive to boys than girls, hence implying some cross-sex typing on the part of girls preferring to play with blocks rather than dolls.

As Kagan and Kogan (1970) have indicated, the published literature strongly supports the view that cross-sex typing is associated with field independence in females. Coates *et al.* (1975) accept this point of view and actually go beyond it to endorse Sherman's (1967) causal hypothesis. The latter position states that extent of practice in spatial visualization tasks influences resultant levels of field independence-dependence.[6] The inference is then drawn by Coates and her colleagues that field independence in girls is enhanced by playing with blocks, a task with a strong component of spatial visualization. Equally credible, however,

[5]This dual aspect of people versus object orientation has also been observed by Jennings (1975). She distinguishes between the child's focus of attention (that is, whether the child's eyes are directed toward people or toward objects) and the context of play (that is, whether the child tends to play alone or with others). Although the two aspects are logically independent, Jennings reports that they are highly and significantly related ($r = .75$). A focus on objects was more likely to occur in a solitary play context; a focus on people was generally associated with group play. The data of Coates *et al.* (1975), however, suggests that the two aspects should be analyzed separately rather than combined into a single index.

[6]In support of Sherman's position is recent evidence indicating that field-dependent 5 year olds' disembedding skill can be markedly improved through a series of perceptual training sessions involving the systematic scanning of increasingly complex figures (see Britain, Dunkel, & Coull, 1975).

is that field-independent girls have achieved that status for other reasons but, by virtue of that status, are drawn to play with blocks. Longitudinal research is clearly needed in order to settle this issue of causal direction. Consideration should also be given to random assignment of preschool children to diverse task content for limited periods of time, although it is evident that such research should not be undertaken without full-scale discussion of the ethical issues involved.

A study highly similar in nature to that of Coates et al. (1975) has been carried out by Jennings (1975), although the construct of field independence-dependence is never cited in the latter work.[7] Jennings inquired whether people vs object orientation in preschoolers would be related to differential intellectual abilities. The former was based on systematic observations obtained in a free play context. The abilities presumed related to object orientation were designated as "tests of physical knowledge" and included three WPPSI scales (Picture Completion, Block Design, and Geometric Design), the latter two of which Coates (1975) found to be strongly related to the PEFT. It is regrettable that Jennings has chosen to include object classification tests (Cattell, 1950; Meyers, Dingman, Orpet, Sitkei, & Watts, 1964) in her physical knowledge composite because such tests do not tap the same kinds of aptitudes represented in the "analytic cluster" of the WPPSI. It is probably more than coincidental, therefore, that the median r among the tests was only .30, with half of the coefficients falling short of significance. Nevertheless, the composite (the major source of variance of which derives from tests strongly related to PEFT performance) did relate significantly ($r = -.41$) to the dimension of people versus object orientation, field-dependent subjects spending relatively more time interacting with people than with objects. Such a correlation also implies, of course, that field-independent subjects spent relatively more time interacting with objects than with people.

Less relevant to the concerns of this volume is Jennings' effort to relate tests of "social knowledge" to people orientation. This relationship was not significant ($r = -.07$), but it is worth noting that this test composite yielded a median r of .22, with two of 15 coefficients significant. Despite this low coherence, the "social knowledge" test composite (which included the WPPSI Comprehension scale and various tasks of role-taking ability, interpersonal perception, and moral judgment) did relate significantly to the child's sociometric popularity among peers and to various personality ratings indicative of leadership, social skills, and self-assertiveness. On the basis of these data, Jennings argues that a "people orientation" does not necessarily imply social competence, and it is the latter that is presumably tapped by tests of "social knowledge."

[7]The indication that different investigators can be working on very similar problems but be unaware of this fact because of the conceptual vantage points from which they begin is a sad commentary on the progressive fragmentation of our discipline.

When Jennings' tests of "physical knowledge" are reinterpreted in field independence-dependence terms, the findings are highly consistent with those of Coates *et al.* (1975) except for the sex difference observed in the latter study. It will be recalled, however, that Coates and her associates retained the distinction between the child's focus of attention in play and the interpersonal context of play, whereas Jennings (on the basis of a .75 correlation) formed a single dimension of people versus object orientation. Conceivably, retention of the two components in a separate analysis for boys and girls would bring the two sets of findings into closer correspondence.

In respect to the matter of causal direction, Jennings acknowledges that it can proceed either way. Preferences for activities with objects can enhance the type of skill required to do well on tests of field independence-dependence (consistent with Sherman's argument); conversely, children who (for reasons of genetic endowment or prior social learning) are inclined toward field independence may therefore orient themselves to the physical rather than the social environment. It is possible, of course, to phrase the above hypotheses in terms of the link between field dependence and people orientation, but only with some difficulty. Whereas the analytic spatial skill reflected in a high level of performance on the WPPSI Block Design scale, for example, bears an obvious relation to some of the toy objects to which preschoolers may be oriented, there is no apparent conceptual connection between a lack of analytic spatial skill and an orientation toward people. It is to Jennings' credit, therefore, that she has tried to construct a composite of tests of social skills, even though the attempt has not been entirely successful. The issue is an important one and is discussed further in Section E of this chapter.

Beyond the research discussed so far, validation studies of the PEFT or other preschool indices of field independence are few in number. In a recent unpublished dissertation, Paul (1975) examined the relationship between separation difficulties and field dependence in a small sample of 3-year-old nursery-school children. Those children classified as making a fairly smooth separation from the parent at the beginning of the nursery-school year were found to score significantly higher on the PEFT than did children who experienced more severe separation problems. It is unfortunate that both the separation ratings and the PEFT administration were carried out by the same investigator, but the fact that the latter followed the former probably served to minimize, if not to eliminate, a biasing effect. Paul's findings are clearly consistent with Witkin's (1964) view that field independence is associated with the development of a sense of separate identity (that is, psychological differentiation from the parent). The unanswered question in Paul's research, however, is whether the child's psychological readiness to separate from the parent is associated with field independence specifically or with cognitive-intellectual development conceived more generally.

D.   SEX DIFFERENCES

Throughout the foregoing discussion of field independence, sex differences have been a prevalent theme. These have often taken the form of significant relationships appearing in one sex but not in the other. Coates' unpublished data strongly suggest that the construct of field independence-dependence has emerged in a coherent form approximately a year earlier in young girls relative to young boys. These findings are highly consistent with the stronger linkages in girls observed in Coates' work between the PEFT index and social behaviors in the nursery-school setting. Unfortunately, Coates' results are not entirely consistent with the outcomes of the Block and Block project, and this discrepancy necessarily detracts from the construct validity of field-independent versus field-dependent cognitive styles in children of preschool age. There is another side to the issue of sex differences, however. We must ask whether 3- to 5-year-old boys and girls differ in mean level of field independence-dependence.

Almost all of the evidence bearing on mean sex differences has been recently reviewed by Coates (1974a). She cites nine studies based on preschool samples, eight of which yielded higher levels of field independence on the PEFT for females than males. For six of these eight, the difference was a statistically significant one. Comparable findings are reported for the mean sex difference on the WPPSI block design subtest. In the data discussed by Coates, the sex difference favoring females was most pronounced at 5 years (Coates, 1974b) and had begun to reverse by 6 years. This is consistent with the CEFT standardization data for children aged 7-12 years, where mean differences, although not statistically significant, nevertheless favored males (Karp & Konstadt, 1963). Significant differences between the sexes on most indices of field independence-dependence are most pronounced during the adolescent secondary-school years. Sex differences in selective college samples are frequently not found (see Kogan, 1976). In short, there is a relatively brief period early in the life span—where female superiority in disembedding skill has been clearly demonstrated. Despite the questionable validity of Oltman's portable rod-and-frame test at the preschool level, it is of considerable interest that the Vaught *et al.* (1975) cross-sectional data (across the age span of 4-13 years) point to male superiority or sex equality with the one exception of 5-year-olds. In this latter age group (and only in this age group) females manifested markedly better performance than males. Note, finally, that sex differences on the draw-a-person task also favored females. Three- to 5-year-old girls yielded significantly higher ABC scores than their male agemates (Ford *et al.*, 1974). Hence, the findings for both RFT and ABC are highly consistent with Coates' summary of the PEFT sex-difference literature. What circumstances prevail during the preschool years to produce the kind of sex difference observed?

Coates (1974a) offers a well-reasoned hypothesis deriving in part from the Maccoby (1966) model in which optimal intellectual functioning is associated with the midpoint of a passivity-activity continuum. The argument advanced by Coates is that girls are closer to this hypothetical midpoint than are boys during the preschool years for reasons having to do with differential motivational dispositions. Evidence is cited (e.g., Coates & Lord, 1973) indicating that preschool girls exceed their male peers in autonomous achievement striving, whereas boys manifest more overt aggression than girls. Furthermore, such aggression was inversely related to both autonomous achievement striving and field independence in boys but was unrelated to those two dimensions in girls. The presumption is made, of course, that autonomous achievement striving in girls represents a shift away from passivity toward a moderate position on the passivity-activity dimension, whereas aggression is at the active extreme where interference with the cognitive processing conducive to field independence can be expected. Beyond the preschool years, girls' passivity is presumed to increase and boys' activity to decrease, hence producing the shifts away from female toward male superiority in disembedding capability.

The foregoing hypothesis has reasonable empirical support and is clearly deserving of further test. As Coates (1974a) has noted, it is particularly important to ascertain the limits of the hypothesis. Is it confined to the cluster of performances that constitute the field-independence construct, or is it a hypothesis equally valid for a wide range of cognitive functioning? Coates also raises the possibility that preschool girls' superiority on disembedding tasks may simply reflect a biologically based higher level of general developmental maturity than has been achieved by boys. An answer to the first question posed above should also prove enlightening with regard to the second.

If the Coates' hypothesis should stand up in the light of further research, the great importance of socialization processes in affecting field-independence levels should be impressed on us. If preschool girls can do better than boys early in the life span, it becomes rather difficult to argue, as do some investigators (e.g., Buffery & Gray, 1972), for the greater genetic potential of males in respect to the spatial-visualization abilities linked to field independence. There is a further point deserving of consideration, however. In the process of constructing an instrument that could be administered to preschoolers, it became necessary to saturate the items with social content (see Fig. 1). Is it possible that female superiority in early childhood can be attributed to that change? It is well known that the standard EFT is strictly geometric and that males tend to excel on it relative to females. Several cogent arguments can be directed against the foregoing explanation. First, the female advantage on the PEFT has vanished by the age of 6 years. Second, the CEFT for older children also contains social content, but males continue to do slightly better. Finally, Block and Block have found a lack of homotypic continuity in girls in the transition from the PEFT to the CEFT, despite the presence of social content in both instruments.

The last of these considerations raises other difficulties, however, for if the same construct is not being assessed in younger and older girls, discussion of sex differences at different ages can only be a fruitless exercise. It would certainly seem to be the case that the continuity issue raised by the Block and Block data must be resolved before the matter of the size and direction of sex differences across age can be genuinely understood.

E.   INFANT PRECURSORS

Given the formal similarity between Kagan's EFT and versions of that test developed for older children, and given the fact that a wealth of data on the infancy period is contained in Kagan's longitudinal study, one can hardly resist the exciting prospect of delineating infant precursors of a field-independent versus field-dependent cognitive style. Regrettably, the relevant findings reported are somewhat disappointing. Of the numerous infant behaviors assessed at 4, 8, and 13 months, only "restless twisting" at 13 months of age was significantly correlated (negatively) with disembedding ability at 27 months, and then only in boys. Moreover, contemporaneous 27-month measures of tempo of free play did not differentiate between low and high EFT scores. It should be noted in all fairness that Kagan and his associates were not really interested in the precursors of field independence-dependence, and hence it is possible that other significant relationships in the data have simply not been reported in their published volume. Those authors were searching primarily for early precursors of reflection-impulsivity (discussed in Chapter III), and their interest focused more on latency to first response on the EFT than on number correct.

A promising direction in the search for infant precursors is suggested by the research of Nelson (1973a) on early language acquisition. Working with children between 1 and 2 years of age, Nelson observed striking individual differences in the degree to which the child's earliest vocabulary was "referential" (that is, largely object oriented) or "expressive" (that is, largely self-oriented). The "referential" children's earliest words were heavily concentrated in the category of general nominals. In contrast, the "expressive" children appeared to acquire words useful for dealing with people (for example, go away, thank you, I want it). Given the link between field independence-dependence and object versus people orientation established in the work of Coates and Jennings described earlier, Nelson's research appears to be of great relevance to the issue of the origins of cognitive styles. Unanswered, of course, is the question of the degree to which these early conceptualizations develop into the cognitive styles of the later preschool period. On the basis of short-term longitudinal followups of the children in her study, Nelson assigns a critical role to the parents' selection and feedback strategies. These can match or mismatch the child's productions, with obvious consequences for both the rate and direction of further cognitive and linguistic development. Detailed examples of such parent-child linguistic interactions are offered by Nelson (1973a, pp. 104-114).

Implicit in the foregoing work is the view that the search for infant precursors does not have to take the exclusive form of direct assessments of the infants themselves. They can concern caretaker activities and the infant's response to the caretaker. Some recent longitudinal data from East Africa focuses on these issues. Munroe and Munroe (1975) report relationships between infant care variables and CEFT performance at 5 years of age in a small sample drawn from the Logoli tribe of Kenya (N varying from 8 to 11 for different measures). Infant care observations began when the infants ranged from 7 to 13 months of age and extended for a period of approximately 4 months. The reported evidence suggested that the degree to which the infant was held by the mother or others had no impact on subsequent CEFT performance. Positive results assumed a somewhat paradoxical form. Where mothers appeared to cause infant crying by departing or ignoring the infant's demands, subsequent CEFT performance (at age 5 years) suffered (to the extent of a significant r of $-.54$). In contrast, where the mother exhibited a longer latency in responding to the infant's cry, subsequent CEFT performance was enhanced (to the extent of a significant r of .70). In sum, it appears as if both infant neglect and oversolicitousness may contribute to depressed CEFT performance (high field dependence). All of the foregoing evidence should be treated with extreme caution, given the wide age range prevailing in the infant sample and the lack of information on the child's behavior between the infancy period and the CEFT administration at 5 years of age. One must also allow for the possibility that the infants' temperamental characteristics in some sense have caused the maternal behaviors (see Bell, 1968; Lewis & Rosenblum, 1974).

F. CONCLUSIONS AND IMPLICATIONS

Despite the apparent contradictions in the accumulated body of data, it would seem fair to conclude that reliable assessment of field independence-dependence in children of preschool age is eminently feasible. Furthermore, these assessments bear theoretically meaningful relationships to preschoolers' behavior in the real world. The preschool pattern does not fit that of older subjects in all particulars, but the demonstration of continuity in a cognitive construct (distinct from IQ) from 2-3 years of age upward through the life span does not seem to be an unreachable goal. The bits and pieces of the puzzle that are available so far point clearly, although not unequivocally, to continuities rather than discontinuities between preschoolers and older children in the psychological significance of field independence-dependence levels. It remains for future research to spell out more precisely the conditions under which discontinuities are most probable. Longitudinal research currently in progress spanning the preschool and early school age periods will almost certainly go a long way toward resolving the ambiguities highlighted in this chapter. If long-term stability down to the preschool period could be established, the empirical exploration of possible infant precursors would become feasible. There has been much speculation by Witkin and others regarding the relative contribution of genetics and socialization to individual variation in field independence-dependence. The search for developmental origins must clearly proceed in two directions—the examination of temperamental and attentional variables in infancy and the study of infant care variables. Research on these issues has barely begun, and we can expect that a simple resolution of the causal direction of effects to be not easily achieved. The indication that parental responses to the infant are partially attributable to the infant's constitutional characteristics (Bell, 1968) enormously complicates the task of delineating infant precursors of field-independent and field-dependent cognitive styles. Nevertheless, our understanding of the developmental origins of cognitive style clearly depends on longitudinal research beginning in infancy. Retrospective accounts by parents of their child-rearing practices (Witkin et al., 1962) are not an effective substitute.[8]

On the basis of the evidence available so far, it appears quite likely that extrapolations downward to the preschool period must be done separately for males and females. As we have seen, sex differences are pervasive at this stage of the life cycle. Not only do we find that later sex differences are reversed—preschool girls may well be more field independent than preschool boys—but sex also seems to act as a moderator variable during this period. Moderated relationships—the observation that diverse indices of field dependence "hang together" (manifest convergent validity) earlier for girls than boys at the preschool level— necessarily imply that the construct makes its appearance at an earlier chronological age in females. It should then follow that correlations between field-independence indices and conceptually related social behaviors can be expected to achieve higher magnitudes in girls than in boys.

Such a moderated sex difference has been obtained in some cases, but the fact that it does not occur uniformly across all studies represents one of the puzzling discrepancies in the data that calls for additional research. It is possible, of course, that the PEFT in preschool boys (although unrelated to RFT and ABC) carries enough valid field-independence variance to yield relationships that approximate, and sometimes even exceed, those observed in girls. There is also an indication in the Block and Block data that PEFT relates more strongly to fluid intelligence (Ravens Progressive Matrices) in boys than in girls. Conceivably, then, field independence is more reflective of sheer intellective power in preschool boys, but is of a more stylistic character in girls. Again, such a

---

[8]Dreyer (1975) has recently begun to examine ongoing family interaction patterns of field-independent and field-dependent kindergarten children. Tentative outcomes of this research indicate that these patterns vary as a function of the cognitive style and sex of the child and, of equal importance, of the setting in which the family interaction is observed (home versus laboratory).

difference could be expected to produce findings more consistent with Witkin's formulations in female as opposed to male samples.

It is to the credit of most of the investigators studying field independence-dependence in preschool children that they have generally included standard measures of intelligence among their research procedures. In much of the research reported, these latter measures have served in a control capacity (as in Coates' partial correlational analyses). This is certainly to be commended, but I cannot help but feel that a stepwise multiple-regression model may be more enlightening. It may be of considerable interest to observe how much incremental variance in particular dependent variables is accounted for by field independence-dependence beyond that portion attributable to such intellective assessors as PPVT, WPPSI, or Ravens Progressive Matrices. Such evidence would help to clarify the matter of the discriminant validity of the field-independence construct at the preschool level, and thereby would provide a valuable supplement to the more extensive information available for convergent validity.[9]

A final concern—one with obvious parallels in older subjects (Vernon, 1972)—rests on the degree to which it is genuinely possible to discriminate the operational indices of field independence—analytic disembedding capacity on spatial tasks—from spatial visualization ability conceived more generally. This may appear to be too subtle a distinction to bother with, but it cannot be ignored if we are to do justice to Witkin's theoretical formulation. It is possible to employ tasks of spatial visualization with preschoolers that do not necessarily call for analytic and/or disembedding skill. The Spatial Relations subtest from the Primary Mental Abilities Test battery (Thurstone & Thurstone, 1963) represents one example. Alternatively, there are the spatial perspective-taking tasks of the type originally developed by Flavell and his associates (Flavell, Botkin, Fry, Wright, & Jarvis, 1968) to assess aspects of decentering. Neither should, on conceptual grounds alone, bear a significant empirical relationship to field independence. Such tasks require spatial visualization but do not require that a form be extracted from a disembedding context. Indeed, one may argue the case that field-dependent children should be better able to appreciate the perceptual perspective afforded by another person in the Flavell et al. (1968) tasks, particularly if the materials employed are of a social or person-oriented nature.

It is evident that 25 years of research on field independence-dependence has not provided us with all of the knowledge that is required for a thorough under-

[9]Weisz, O'Neill, and O'Neill (1975) argue that mental age (rather than IQ) is the appropriate control variable for field independence-dependence research based on children. With chronological and mental ages of 9 and 12 years entered as orthogonal factors, these authors were able to show that MA (and not CA) accounted for large portions of the variance in CEFT scores. Furthermore, IQ variation was of no significance with MA controlled. Although the Weisz et al. (1975) research is based on school-age children, its applicability may conceivably extend down to the preschool period. The study that can settle the issue has not yet been carried out.

standing of the construct. Gaps continue to exist, particularly where preschool children are concerned. At the same time, the fact that research on field independence shows no signs of waning after a quarter of a century surely testifies to the fertility of the construct that Witkin and his associates have offered to us. Such "staying power" is a tribute in its own right; criticism loses some of its potency within the context of this long-term perspective.

III

Reflection—Impulsivity

A. GENERAL BACKGROUND

Unlike the history of the field-independence construct, which grew out of research with adults and later was extended to children, the cognitive style of reflection-impulsivity from the very beginning has been almost exclusively child based. Initially conceptualized and operationalized in a monograph by Kagan, Rosman, Day, Albert, and Phillips (1964), the reflection-impulsivity dimension has enjoyed a decade of enormous popularity, and new researches continue to appear with regularity in the journals of developmental and educational psychology. Previously published reviews of this literature (Kagan & Kogan, 1970; Kogan, 1971) are already somewhat dated in the light of the sheer volume of relevant material published in recent years. It is not the aim of this chapter, however, to bring these earlier reviews up to date. A recent review by Messer (1976) has accomplished that objective. This chapter is focused on the infancy and preschool period. The large majority of studies discussed in the previously published reviews concern children of school age. Research based on younger children, in large part, is of more recent vintage and so has not received the integrative treatment previously accorded to work using older children as subjects. It should be noted that there is currently controversy over the issue of whether reflection-impulsivity has the same psychological meaning in both younger and older children (Block, Block, & Harrington, 1974, 1975; Kagan & Messer, 1975). The matter of continuity vs discontinuity of cognitive styles is, of course, central to the mission of this chapter and receives thorough consideration in respect to reflection-impulsivity in the pages that follow.

Kagan and Kogan (1970) define reflection-impulsivity as "concerned with the degree to which the subject reflects on the validity of his solution hypotheses

31

in problems that contain response uncertainty [p. 1309]." The instrument that is most typically employed to assess the present cognitive style is the Matching Familiar Figures test (MFF). Each item on this test consists of a standard and six variants, one of which is identical to the standard. The child is requested to select the matching variant. Response latency to the first hypothesis and number of errors committed constitute the two scores of interest. In school-age children (approximately 6-12 years old), errors decline and response times increase with age, and the relationship between the two indices is consistently negative, rs usually ranging between $-.4$ and $-.6$. Longer response times are associated with a smaller number of errors and shorter response times with a larger number of errors.

B.   ASSESSMENT IN PRESCHOOL CHILDREN

1.   Match-to-Sample Tasks for Preschoolers

Although the MFF has been employed with preschool children (e.g., Harrison & Nadelman, 1972), some investigators believe that the test is too difficult for that age group.[1] Lewis, Rausch, Goldberg, and Dodd (1968) describe a matching-figure task where only four variants are used and their general discriminability is greater than that of the variants employed in the original MFF items. Another version (Banta, 1970), designated the Early Childhood Matching Familiar Figures test (EC-MFF) employs only three variants with each standard. Still another version, the Kansas Reflection-Impulsivity Scale for Preschoolers (KRISP), has been developed by Wright (1971a, 1973) for use primarily with children of preschool age. The latter has now been administered to more than 900 preschoolers in the United States and abroad. The KRISP and an accompanying manual (Wright, 1971a, 1973) are readily available to researchers, and performance norms for children in the age range of 3-6 years are being developed in a systematic manner. An illustrative item from the KRISP and the notebook format of administration are shown in Figs. 2 and 3.

No research has yet been reported in which the Lewis and co-workers, Banta, or Wright versions of the MFF have been related to each other or to Kagan's original MFF. The relationship is quite likely to be positive in the light of evidence reported elsewhere (Yando & Kagan, 1970) of the interindividual stability of reflection-impulsivity indices as the number of variants is permitted to increase incrementally from 2 to 12. At the same time, however, the contradictions in research evidence (reported later in Sections B.5 and D) may well stem from the use of different match-to-sample tasks.

---

[1]Messer (1975) asserts that three forms of the MFF are now available appropriate for preschoolers, school-aged children, and adults, respectively.

FIG. 2   Sample item from the Kansas Reflection-Impulsivity Scale for Preschoolers (KRISP).

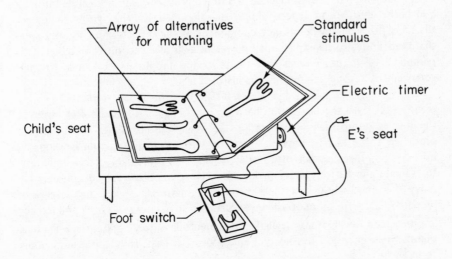

FIG. 3   Apparatus for display of KRISP items.

2. The Combined Error-Latency Index: Critique and Defense

Early in the program of research on reflection-impulsivity initiated by Kagan, a combined error-latency index was introduced—reflectives including children above the sample median on latency and below the median on errors, and impulsives consisting of children below the sample median on latency and above the median on errors. Kagan and his co-workers maintained that the combined index was justified on the basis of the consistently significant and negative association obtained between latency and errors in all of the prior research. Furthermore, the Kagan group particularly wished to distinguish two classes of children with fast response times—those making many errors and those making few errors. In other words, impulsiveness was deliberately defined as maladaptive in nature. The inclusion of the accuracy component in the index of reflection-impulsivity necessarily implies that we are here dealing with a Type I cognitive style as described in Chapter I.

A direct consequence of the use of the foregoing combined index has been the elimination of a substantial number of subjects from further analysis in empirical studies of reflection-impulsivity. These are the children with relatively slow response times who make numerous errors—the slow inaccurates—and those with relatively rapid response times who make few errors—the fast accurates. Block et al. (1974) are highly critical of the concentration on two of the four latency-error cells and, in fact, question the designation of the two chosen cells in reflection-impulsivity terms.[2] Those authors take the position that level of accuracy may be a consequence of a reflective versus impulsive style but may also be attributable to general ability or other factors. They go on to suggest that it is the accuracy-inaccuracy component of the reflection-impulsivity style that contributes to its explanatory power vis-à-vis other cognitive variables. This reasoning, of course, implies that the reflection-impulsivity label used to characterize MFF responding may not be justified.

The response of Kagan and Messer (1975) to the Block et al. (1974) argument emphasized the distinction between school-age and preschool children. In the former group, inverse correlations between response times and errors are presumed to be higher, implying that the MFF is clearly tapping a task-based information-processing activity. Reflective subjects presumably take ample time to evaluate alternatives, hence making few errors; impulsive subjects presumably hurry their evaluation and thereby make numerous mistakes. In the case of preschool children, by contrast, inverse correlations between errors and latency are presumed lower, if not negligible, in magnitude, implying that the reflection-impulsivity dimension has not yet emerged or, at best, is in quite rudimentary form.[3]

[2]Note that Eska and Black (1971) and Ault, Crawford, and Jeffrey (1972) were the first investigators to include fast accurates and slow inaccurates along with reflectives and impulsives in data analyses of school-aged children.

[3]Kagan has not always expressed such pessimism regarding the assessment of reflection-

There are at least two difficulties with the Kagan-Messer position. First, if one examines the samples reporting the highest negative correlations for school-age children, the proportion of subjects unequivocally classified as reflective or impulsive by the median-split procedure never exceeds three-quarters of the sample (see Ward, 1973a). It is clear, then, that a substantial percentage of older school-age children cannot readily be accommodated under the reflection-impulsivity rubric as operationally defined by Kagan and his colleagues. Secondly, although inverse correlations between errors and latency do run somewhat lower for preschool relative to school-age children, one does not discern a sharp split in correlational magnitudes between these discrepant age groups (see Block *et al.*, 1975). Hence, there seems to be a reasonable proportion of preschool children for whom the reflection-impulsivity dimension is no less relevant than for older school-age children.

It must be acknowledged in support of Kagan and Messer that there are preschool samples where reported correlations between response time and errors are negligible (e.g., Banta, 1970; Ward, 1973b; Wright, 1972).[4] Block *et al.* (1975) dismiss these studies as irrelevant to the controversy on the grounds that the preschool children employed as subjects have been of low socioeconomic status, hence invalidating comparisons with older middle-class children. It would seem that Block *et al.* (1975) have pushed their argument a bit too far, however, for in the case of the higher SES 4-year-olds studied by Ward (1973b) as well as the middle-class 3- and 4-year-old females studied by Wright (1972), response time and latency were unrelated. Indeed, the latter two variables were uncorrelated for 3-year-olds in the Blocks' own unpublished data. Most of the relevant studies suggest the presence of a critical period during the preschool years in respect to match-to-sample performance. At the earlier age, response time has no apparent connection with error; 1 year later in the same samples, the significant inverse relationship between response time and errors is manifest. Ward (1973b) has also shown that this relationship, when finally emergent, is independent of general ability.

3.   Changes in Construct Meaning during the Preschool Period

Ward's data indicate that SES affects the timing of the transition, not whether the transition as such does occur. For higher SES children, the transition period may occur as much as a year earlier than is observed in children lower in

---

impulsivity in preschool children. In an earlier paper (Kagan, 1967), the construct is applied to children as young as 4 years of age.

[4]Even in these cases, however, approximately 50% of the sample can be labeled as reflective or impulsive, and they have in fact been so labeled. This introduces the difficult question of how high the correlation between latency and errors has to be before the use of median splits for classification can be justified. Is bare statistical significance sufficient, for example, given its direct dependence on sample size?

SES.[5] Data reported by Lewis *et al.* (1968) and Wright (1972) suggest that the transition may take place even earlier than 3-4 years of age. Hence, regardless of SES, there is a discontinuity in the meaning of the reflection-impulsivity dimension within the preschool period. This is bound to have important consequences in any longitudinal search for infant precursors of reflection-impulsivity. Given the homotypic discontinuity characteristic of the preschool period, one would have little reason to expect similar infant precursors for preschool children assessed in the MFF at 3 and at 5 years of age, for example. The same logic should necessarily apply to concurrent correlates of reflection-impulsivity. One does not expect the same relationships with other variables to obtain in younger preschool children, for whom latency and errors are functionally unconnected, and in older preschool children, for whom the functional link has been established.

An important methodological issue is raised by Ward (1973a) in respect to the meaning of a modest but significant inverse correlation between response time and errors. One possibility is that of a fairly uniform weak association across subjects for the two variables of interest. The other possibility, the more viable one in fact, is that the two variables are firmly related on some functional basis in certain children and not related at all in other children. Hence, the increase in the magnitude of the correlation with age indicates a progressive increase over time in the proportion of children for whom latency and errors become functionally interconnected. Pursuing this line of reasoning further, it would appear that Kagan's earlier decision to work only with two of the four cells produced by the median-split technique, the fast inaccurates and the slow accurates, has a reasonable theoretical justification. This does not imply, as Block *et al.* (1974, 1975) have asserted, that reflection-impulsivity represents the most judicious choice of label for characterizing the dimension. Nor can the exclusion of the remaining two subgroups of children from theoretical and empirical consideration be justified. Where the preschool period is of primary concern, the slow inaccurates and the fast accurates represent a large chunk of the samples under study, and it is obviously important to understand why they respond as they do.

Ward (1973a, b) argues that those children who have not brought response time and errors into a functional linkage when coping with the MFF are governed by considerations of response tempo and general ability. The slow inaccurate is presumed to be a slow-tempo child of relatively low ability. The fast accurate is considered a rapid-tempo child of relatively high ability. There is no apparent theoretical basis for expecting general response tempo and level of ability to manifest a relationship and, in fact, Ward (1973b) has found none.

---

[5]It is acknowledged that SES as such is not a psychological variable and, hence, to attribute an effect to SES represents a starting point rather than an end point for explanation (see also Block, 1971).

If children's latency on MFF is a reflection of general response tempo and not of specific information-processing requirements of the MFF, such latencies should correlate with latencies obtained from other tasks that do not have the response-uncertainty feature characteristic of the MFF test. Ward (1973b) addresses himself to this question, using latencies to first response on the Sigel Object Categorization Test (see Lindstrom & Shipman, 1972) and the PEFT. In the ETS longitudinal study, rs between MFF and Sigel latencies were .46, .07, and .29 for 4-, 5-, and 6-year-old children, respectively. Ward argues that the relatively high r for the 4-year-olds points to the general response-tempo factor at work. The correlation is negligible in the 5-year-olds because some children at this age are alert to the special information-processing requirements of the MFF, thereby reducing the impact of response tempo ,as such. The correlation rises again in the 6-year-olds, according to Ward, because children are now aware of the alternative grouping possibilities on the Sigel task, implying that the latter now also possesses the response-uncertainty aspect of the MFF. The viability of this interpretation rests on the assumption, not directly tested, that children do not acquire the necessary information-processing skills for the MFF and the Sigel task at approximately the same time.

The correlations between MFF and PEFT response times were .18, .10, and .18 in the 4-, 5-, and 6-year-olds, respectively. These outcomes are less supportive of the general hypothesis. If a pervasive response tempo factor is salient in the 4-year-olds, it is difficult to comprehend the quite low correlation observed in that age group. At the same time, the PEFT is not a task that is clearly distinguished by response uncertainty, and so the relatively low rs obtained in the older children do not disturb Ward's hypothesis.

4.   Stability of Assessments

Consider next the consistency of the response time and error components of MFF performance during the preschool years. In the Block and Block research, the response time consistency coefficients over a 1-year period (ages 3-4 years) were .28 and .13 (neither statistically significant) for boys and girls, respectively. The corresponding coefficients for errors were .43 and .46 (both significant at the .01 level). Ward's (1973b) stability coefficients extended over a 3-year period and were highly similar to the Block and Block outcomes. Coefficients for stability of latencies ranged from .13 to .24; for stability of errors, the range was from .34 to .51. In sum, error scores were substantially more stable than latencies.[6] This discrepancy in stability between errors and latencies has direct

[6]Wright's (1972) data (based on a small sample of 19 boys and 21 girls administered the KRISP at 3 and 4 years of age) are discrepant from those reported above. Males were not consistent on either time or error dimensions (rs of −.16 and .09, respectively); females were consistent on both (rs of .67 and .42, respectively). The relatively small Ns involved suggests that these findings be held in abeyance until additional data are collected.

developmental implications. If the developmental course is one in which laten-cies and errors shift from relative independence to a functionally based inverse relation, the stability of error rates necessarily implies that latencies must eventually change in a direction consistent with error tendencies. Ward (1973a) provides evidence supportive of the foregoing inference. When the 5-year-olds in the ETS longitudinal study were divided into those who manifested the inverse association between latency and errors and those who did not, only the former children manifested latency stability at 6 years of age. In short, latencies achieve stability when the child can be truly located on the "reflection-impulsiv-ity" stylistic dimension, but they are quite unstable prior to that time.

5.   Developmental Mean Differences

Consistent with the evidence of increasing latencies and decreasing error scores over the early school-age years (Kagan, 1966), Ward (1973b) found a similar linear pattern for both of the MFF components during the preschool years (3-6 years of age). Block and Block also obtained significant increases in latency and declines in errors for both boys and girls between the ages of 3 and 4 years. Similarly, Wright (1972) found that errors on the KRISP declined significantly between 3 and 5 years of age. In the case of KRISP latencies, little change was obtained between 3 and 4 years of age, but a significant decrease was observed at 5 years of age. The latter finding is markedly discrepant from Ward's data and from the general developmental trend. The discrepancy forces consideration of the comparability of MFF and KRISP performance during the preschool years.

C.   VALIDATION AT THE PRESCHOOL LEVEL

We turn finally to the important issue of the construct validity of a reflective vs impulsive style in preschool children. At the more descriptive or phenomenal level of performance on the MFF or other similar tasks distinguished by response uncertainty, there can be no doubt that the reflective style represents a capacity or willingness to delay or inhibit a response in the service of seeking an accurate solution to a problem. In contrast, the impulsive style (in Kagan's sense of short response times and error proneness) necessarily implies an incapacity or un-willingness to delay or inhibit a response in the interest of problem solution. With delay or inhibition as the primary consideration, it is clear that the reflec-tion-impulsivity dimension has much to do with self-regulatory behavior.

The question of construct validity can be pursued at two levels. The first inquires directly about the underlying cognitive processes that account for individual variations in performance on match-to-sample tasks. Such tasks demand active visual scanning in the service of information processing. These scanning strategies can obviously vary in efficiency (as indexed by eye-movement patterns), and one naturally wants to know how differences between reflectives and impulsives are manifested at that basic cognitive level. The second construct-validational approach derives directly from the self-regulation idea and involves the examination of associations between reflection-impulsivity on match-to-sample tasks and other indicators of delay or inhibition, where these are required by the task at issue.

Construct validity must also be pursued at the deeper level of understanding the basis for delay or inhibition in problem-solving situations containing response uncertainty. Here, considerable ambiguity has resulted as a consequence of the different explanations of dynamics offered by Kagan and his colleagues (e.g., Kagan *et al.,* 1964; Kagan & Kogan, 1970) to account for a reflective vs an impulsive performance on the MFF test and other tasks containing response uncertainty. Most recently, Kagan has seemed to lean toward a straightforward anxiety over error dynamic, the reflective being high and the impulsive low on this particular characteristic. Earlier, however, Kagan gave much credibility to the possibility of qualitatively different sources of anxiety in reflectives and impulsives—the former experiencing anxiety over making a mistake on a task considered essentially manageable, the latter experiencing anxiety over delaying a response in a context where task competence is in question. Assuming that Kagan would be more favorably inclined toward his more recent explanation of reflection-impulsivity dynamics, Block *et al.* (1974) used it as a major point of attack on Kagan's conceptualization. Construct validity in the terms of Block and his co-workers requires that the personality characteristics of children deemed reflective or impulsive on the MFF test be compatible with the cognitive dynamics attributed to both poles of the stylistic dimension. The observed disparity between purported dynamics and personality characteristics (assessed via the *Q* sort technique) are thoroughly considered later (Section III.F). First, however, let us examine the evidence on eye-movement patterns in relation to reflection-impulsivity.

1. Visual Scanning Patterns

McCluskey and Wright (1973) are the only investigators to examine the visual scanning behavior of reflective and impulsive children of preschool age. That study included 40 subjects equally divided by sex and age (half were 3 and half were 5 years of age, on the average). Designation of the child as reflective or impulsive was based on scores derived from the KRISP.

The test stimuli employed for the study of the children's eye movements consisted of two rows of three figures each. The figures (e.g., a child holding a balloon) in each row were aligned directly on top of one another. The middle figures were always identical, but the figures on either the left or the right (randomized across stimuli) differed from each other. The child was requested to report where the difference occurred. During the performance of this task, the child's face was videotaped. The tapes were used to score the eye movements of each subject. Two independent scorers were in substantial agreement in the eye-movement scoring (reliabilities ranging from .80 to .95 with a mean of .91).

Although the McCluskey and Wright research is quite ingenious in its development of apparatus to measure preschoolers' eye movements, one cannot help but be puzzled by the use of a task that requires the detection of a difference rather than a similarity. As a match-to-sample task, the KRISP requires that the child locate the variant identical to the standard. Searching for a difference and searching for a similarity entail different kinds of search strategies (see Zelniker, Jeffrey, Ault, & Parsons, 1972). This contrast may account for the relatively low nonsignificant correlation ($r = .24$) between response times on the KRISP and the eye-movement task.

Within the limitations cited, let us proceed to an examination of the findings. Several eye-movement scores were obtained. These included total looks (that is, overall number of fixations), middle looks (that is, fixations at uninformative middle figures), nonhomologous comparisons (that is, horizontal and diagonal shifts of fixation), and homologous comparisons (that is, vertical shifts of fixation). The last of these were further subdivided into informative comparisons (that is, those at stimulus ends where differences occurred) and uninformative comparisons (that is, those at stimulus center where differences never occurred).

In respect to homologous comparisons, significant F ratios were obtained for age and reflection-impulsivity, older and reflective children generating a larger number of such comparisons. Comparable significant effects were obtained for informative homologous comparisons. Older and reflective children also made significantly fewer errors on the eye-movement task, but response time was associated with age (older children responding more slowly), not with reflection-impulsivity. Sex differences also have been found, but these are discussed in Section III, D. In sum, both age and reflection contributed to the use of visual scanning strategies that are adaptive in a task requiring the detection of differences.

Elsewhere, Wright (1971b) has speculated about age-related changes in eye-movement patterns. He proposes that the developmental sequence is distinguished by three stages, starting with unsystematic minimal scanning, proceeding to a concentration on the standard in which each alternative is regularly checked against it, and terminating with systematic scanning of the array of alternatives to ascertain critical features prior to checking against the standard. In Wright's view, reflective children pass through the developmental sequence more rapidly than do impulsive children. This would imply that a first-grade reflective might resemble a fourth-grade impulsive, for example. Evidence in support of the foregoing position for older children and adults is reported by Siegelman (1969) and Drake (1970) and for younger children by Wright (1971b). More recent work, however, has indicated that the fundamental scanning difference between fourth-grade reflectives and impulsives is that the former simply return more often to previously fixated stimuli (Ault et al., 1972; Zelniker et al., 1972). In sum, the evidence in support of Wright's proposed developmental sequence is far from definitive at the present time.

If reflectives and impulsives can be distinguished on the basis of the extent of systematic scanning of the critical features of stimuli, such a difference should also be reflected in the performance of those two classes of subjects on other relevant cognitive tasks. In a recent study based on 16 black preschool children (Siegel, Kirasic, & Kilburg, 1973), reflection-impulsivity (assessed with the KRISP) was observed to relate to performance on a task of recognition memory. Children successively scanned a set of 80 stimuli (pictures of familiar objects). Immediately thereafter, they were shown 80 test cards, each containing two pictures, one of which had been included in the initial stimulus set.[7] The instructions to the children requested that they point out the picture they had seen before. The set of 80 test stimuli were divided into subsets that varied in anticipated difficulty dependent on the nature of the incorrect member of the pair—a picture from a different object class or a picture from the same object class but varying in detail(s). It was assumed that the latter would prove more difficult for preschoolers because accuracy depended on a thorough feature analysis of the original stimulus. In contrast, accuracy on the former is insured if correct verbal labeling has taken place.

The results of the research by Siegel and his co-workers indicated that reflectives' recognition memory was generally better than that of impulsives across the board. In other words, the reflective children displayed better recognition memory than did impulsive children, irrespective of whether the specific items required verbal labeling or a thorough feature analysis. In this respect, the results only partially support the general hypothesis, for a reflective KRISP performance has little to do with adequate verbal labeling. It is regrettable that a general intelligence control was not included in the research. The evidence that reflectives performed better than impulsives on difficult items in all conditions (verbal labeling and feature analysis) certainly points to the possible influence of something resembling a "g" factor.

2.   Relation to Other Self-Regulatory Behaviors

Consider next an alternative approach to the construct validation of reflection-impulsivity. Does it enter into a meaningful network of correlations with other variables? A first requirement is that the MFF relate to other tasks having the

[7] For 20 of the pictures, the test stimulus pairs did not include the actual picture seen previously by the child but a different picture belonging to the same general object class. According to Siegel et al. (1973), the "condition was included to see how children's recognition memory functioned for stimuli that they had never seen before but for which they might have either a global template or name from the presentation deck [p. 653]."

property of response uncertainty. Whereas such generality appears to exist in school-age children (Kagan *et al.*, 1964; Kagan, 1965; Mann, 1973; Odom, McIntyre, & Neale, 1971), although not without exception (Eska & Black, 1971), only one investigation (Ward, 1968b) has confirmed the presence of generality (convergent validity) in preschool (kindergarten) children. Because no contrary evidence exists, however, it seems reasonable to assume at least limited generality in preschoolers for the time being so that we can proceed to the next major item of importance. Does MFF performance relate to behavior on other tasks that have a self-regulatory although not a response-uncertainty character?

A most obvious task of the foregoing sort is the motor inhibition test (MIT) devised by Maccoby, Dowley, Hagen, and Degerman (1965) for use with preschool children. Three simple motor tasks were first given to the subjects for practice, to permit an assessment of the child's customary pace in completing the task. Then, instructions were given to complete the same tasks as slowly as possible. The children, in other words, had to inhibit normal muscle movement in order to perform well. The three tasks were found to be highly reliable and substantially intercorrelated in both sexes, suggesting that motor inhibition constitutes a generalized disposition in its own right. Stability of MIT performance in preschoolers over a 1- and a 2-year period is reported by Block and Block and by Ward (1973b), respectively. These motor tasks have also been given to preschool children to perform as quickly as possible (Massari, Hayweiser, & Meyer, 1969). The lack of any relation between scores obtained under "slow" and "fast" instructions suggests that sheer ability to comprehend experimental instructions is not at issue. Instead, children who slow down the most when instructed to do so are those most able or willing to inhibit motor movement.

Is the cognitive inhibition required for effective performance on response-uncertainty tasks, such as MFF, related to the motoric inhibition required to slow down on tasks such as those included in the MIT? Evidence for a moderate significant relationship has been reported in the case of school-age samples (Ward, 1968a), and this finding has since been replicated in preschool children. In their sample of black middle-class preschoolers (ranging in age from 4 to 5 years), Harrison and Nadelman (1972) obtained significant correlations in the expected direction in both sexes between MFF latency and error scores, on the one hand, and the magnitude of slowing down on the MIT, on the other. Banta (1970), who did not score his version of the MFF for latency, also reported a significant positive correlation between MFF errors and less slowing on the MIT in a sample of lower class black preschoolers. On the negative side, Mumbauer and Miller (1970) found no MFF-MIT relationships in a study of 4- to 6-year-old children of mixed SES. Block and Block also did not obtain a clear pattern of relationships. In the case of 3- and 4-year-old middle-class children, MFF latencies were uniformly unrelated to MIT "slow" scores. Only for the 3-year-old boys was a relationship apparent between MFF errors and slowness on the MIT (corrected for baseline slowness). It should be noted that such a correction factor was not used by Banta (1970) or by Harrison and Nadelman (1972).

Still another factor that must be considered in evaluating the MFF-MIT relationship is the role of general ability in mediating whatever significant associations are found. Ward (1973b) reports significant negative correlations between MFF errors and slowness on the MIT at each age level—4, 5, and 6 years—in the ETS longitudinal study. Yet when general ability as indexed by Caldwell's Preschool Inventory (see Gilbert & Shipman, 1972) was controlled in a partial correlational analysis, the MFF-MIT correlations turned negligible and nonsignificant at each age level. MFF latency was not associated with MIT slowness in children assessed at 4 and 5 years, but a positive relation emerged in these children when they were tested at 6 years of age. The latter relation remained statistically significant with general ability controlled. In sum, general ability variance accounts for linkages between MFF error and MIT slowness, but as development proceeds to the point where latencies have a clear information-processing function, these now enter into a significant positive relationship with capacity or willingness to slow down on the motor inhibition test.

3. Relation to Intelligence Assessments

The discussion so far has focused on convergent validation. Attention must also be paid to discriminant validity, of course, and, in cognitive-style research, this has typically concerned the extent of the relationship to intelligence. Messer (1976) has surveyed the relevant evidence for both preschool and school-age children. Examination of that evidence in preschoolers indicates an inconsistent pattern of correlations between MFF response time and IQ indices. Across 10 samples of 3- to 5-year-old children of varying SES, rs have ranged from −.03 to .52 (median r of .25).[8] The relation between MFF error scores and IQ appears to be much more consistent and substantial in the same 10 samples (rs ranging from −.21 to −.63, with a median r of −.51). In fact, in the light of the internal-consistency reliabilities of MFF error scores (typically in the 50s), it would not be too far fetched to assert that the MFF error score in preschoolers can be treated as an alternate form of an IQ test. A more ambiguous situation prevails in the case of MFF response time, however.

Messer (1976) has posed the interesting hypothesis that the size of the MFF response time-IQ correlation depends on the specific type of intelligence test employed. Such tests can place a premium on productive verbal skill (as in WPPSI verbal scales) or on capacity to choose the correct answer from among

[8]In computing the median r from Messer's (1976) Table 4, rs for males and females combined were used. When a combined r was not reported, the average of the rs for males and females was employed. This procedure was followed for both MFF response times and errors.

several response alternatives (usually of a pictorial form in preschool tests). The latter are presumed to have more of the response-uncertainty properties characteristic of the MFF than do the former and so are expected to yield higher correlations with MFF scores. Messer had four judges categorize the various intelligence tests used in reflection-impulsivity research according to whether they would generate correlations with MFF response time falling above or below the median correlation. For seven of the 10 IQ tests at issue, all four judges agreed in their categorization. When these categorizations were then compared with the actual findings, a significant chi-square ensued, indicating that IQ tests judged to be similar to the MFF entered into higher correlations with the MFF response-time index. This outcome is highly reminiscent of the differential relation between field independence and diverse intelligence tests discussed in Chapter II. Findings such as these are exceedingly important for they call into question the oft-presumed causal priority of IQ in respect to indices of cognitive style. There is little reason to doubt that the kind of cognitive strategy elicited by the MFF (as well as by other measures of cognitive style) can influence the cognitive approach employed on an intelligence test. It would be most surprising if such variations in cognitive approach had no effect on intelligence test scores.

Particularly puzzling is Messer's (1976) failure to carry out a comparable analysis for MFF error scores. Although these relate more strongly to IQ indices than do latencies, the range of correlations is quite broad (extending from near zero into the 60s across all age groups). The lack of such an analysis necessarily implies that our comprehension of MFF-IQ relations is less than complete. The issue of the discriminant validity of reflection-impulsivity vis-á-vis intelligence level is therefore left in a state of limbo.

4. Relation to Cognitive Developmental Level

A strikingly different slant on the discriminant validity issue is contained in a recent paper by Achenbach and Weisz (1975). It is the contention of those authors that IQ (an index of ability relative to one's age mates) is not the ideal control variable for use with young children. Instead, Achenbach and Weisz maintain that the critical task is to determine how much of the variance in reflection-impulsivity is attributable to its status as a trait construct and how much to its status as an index of overall cognitive developmental level. Mental age (MA) is considered to be the best indicator of the latter and hence is used by Achenbach and Weisz in their discriminant validity study.

The study itself was longitudinal in character. Nursery-school and day care children (55 boys and 47 girls) were tested for reflection-impulsivity (KRISP) and mental age (Stanford-Binet). Retesting on both took place 6 months later. At the latter time, a measure of hypothesis behavior based on Levine's (1966) "blank trials" procedure was also obtained. In respect to results, whether concurrent or cross-time relations are considered, the magnitude of the correlations were uniformly and (in the large majority of the cases) significantly higher for KRISP vis-á-vis MA than for KRISP vis-á-vis IQ. Further, only 11% of the variance in reflection-impulsivity at the second testing could be uniquely accounted for on the basis of the first reflection-impulsivity assessment; the latter combined with mental age levels obtained from both testings accounted for an additional 33.5% of the variance in the second reflection-impulsivity measurement. Finally, the significant predictability of hypothesis behavior from reflection-impulsivity status ceased to hold when mental age was covaried in an analysis of covariance.

The Achenbach-Weisz study is of particular significance for research on cognitive styles in children of preschool age. Cognitive developmental change probably proceeds more rapidly during the preschool period than is the case for later childhood, and hence a 6-month interval offers more opportunity for cognitive growth in a nursery-school group than is the case for a sample of elementary-school children. This implies that MA may well prove to be a more relevant control variable than is IQ in early childhood. A great deal of prior research requires reconsideration if the Achenbach-Weisz position is a genuinely valid one. Those authors have convincingly shown, in fact, that earlier research (Katz, 1971) attributing form and color choices in a color-form sorting task to reflection and impulsivity, respectively, can be essentially reinterpreted to take account of the dominant explanatory status of general developmental level.

Achenbach and Weisz (1975) have offered a strong case in support of mental age as the most meaningful control variable in studies of the discriminant validity of the reflection-impulsivity construct. It is not an ironclad case, however. Particularly puzzling is the rather consistent evidence offered in the Messer (1976) review of significant (and often highly substantial) relations between MFF error scores and IQ indices in preschool children. Conceivably, of course, the substitution of MA level in all of those studies would have led to marked enhancement of correlations with MFF errors. There is good reason to doubt this, however. The evidence appears to point to the generalization that IQ has a diminishing effect, and MA a progressively enhancing effect, on reflection-impulsivity measures as the chronological age (CA) range of the subject sample increases. For example, the CA range in the Achenbach-Weisz study (35-74 months) is possibly the largest ever employed in reflection-impulsivity research, and the correlations of IQ with latency and error scores are among the smallest reported. The CA range is so broad, in fact, that one does not expect much of a change in the outcomes of the Achenbach-Weisz research if CA should be substituted for MA in their analyses. Indeed, these authors' critique of Katz's (1971) research (where CA ranged from 44 to 65 months) was based on the fact that CA correlated significantly in the expected direction with MFF latencies and errors and with form as opposed to color responding.[9]

[9] A subsequent article by Katz (1972) demonstrated that impulsive preschoolers were

(Footnote 9 continued on page 46)

Where the CA range in preschool samples has not exceeded 12-13 months, correlations of IQ with both latency and error scores have been highly significant (Lewis *et al.*, 1968; Meichenbaum & Goodman, 1969; Mumbauer & Miller, 1970). However, two studies (Massari & Massari, 1973; Ward, 1968b) in which the CA range exceeded 24 months yielded marginal MFF-IQ correlations of about the same magnitude as reported in Achenbach and Weisz (1975). The one exception to the foregoing contrast in the published literature is a study by Harrison and Nadelman (1972). Even though the latter authors employed a sample with a CA range not exceeding 12 months, the relevant correlations with IQ, although in the expected direction, were marginal in magnitude.

The foregoing analysis is not intended to detract from the Achenbach and Weisz contribution. Developmental level will clearly covary with cognitive style indices in preschool samples characterized by relatively broad age spans (in the vicinity of 2 years or more). Researchers working with preschoolers must either take statistical account of this factor or constitute their samples to yield greater age homogeneity. Dividing a preschool sample into younger and older subgroups should provide an effective control for developmental level (although not for IQ). Alternatively, one could enter CA and MA as orthogonal factors in the design of the study, the technique employed by Weisz *et al.* (1975) for the field-independence dimension.

When level of cognitive development is indexed as mental age (MA), one should not lose sight of the fact that we are dealing with a global score on an intelligence test. Despite the strong temptation to assign causal priority to the latter, there is little justification for doing so. It is just as feasible for cognitive styles and strategies to affect intellective test performance as for the latter to influence the former. With longitudinal data of the type gathered by Achenbach and Weisz, it is possible to apply some of the newer techniques, such as path analysis (Heise, 1969) or cross-lagged panel correlational analysis (e.g., Rozelle & Campbell, 1969). Although these techniques are hardly foolproof, they offer the possibility of getting some hold on the causal linkages between ability and style variables. This is one of the major unsettled issues in the area, and its clarification would represent a breakthrough of the utmost importance.

D.   SEX DIFFERENCES

On the issue of sex differences in MFF performance, no systematic effect has emerged in school-age children. Where preschool children are concerned, mean sex differences for MFF latencies and errors and for MIT slowness have not appeared in every study. When differences do occur, however, they almost always are in the direction of greater impulsiveness in boys (see Maccoby &

---

less able than their reflective peers to note relatively gross form differences in a simple discrimination task. This study, however, is based on the same subjects employed in Katz (1971) and hence is open to the same criticism.

Jacklin, 1974). Of possibly greater interest than a difference in level, however, is evidence presented by Ward (1973b) suggesting that the functional connection between MFF latencies and errors shows up approximately 1 year earlier in females than in males. For 5 year olds, the correlations were $-.01$ and $-.20$ for males and females, respectively. Regrettably, the pattern of sex differences on the KRISP runs directly counter to Ward. In subsamples ranging from 32 to 78 in size, Wright (1972) found significant latency-error correlations for 3-, 4-, and 5-year-old males (rs of $-.44$, $-.36$, and $-.27$, respectively). In the case of the females, the corresponding rs were $-.08$, $-.11$, and $-.22$, respectively. Only the last of these achieved statistical significance. Such contrary findings clearly muddy the issue of sex differences and may well be a consequence of the use of different instruments for tapping identical constructs.

Although the findings reported by Wright (1972) suggest that girls may be less developmentally advanced than boys, other evidence from that research project points to the very opposite conclusion. Correlations between 3- and 4-year-old KRISP performance for 19 males were $-.16$ for response time and $.09$ for errors. Comparable correlations for 21 females were $.67$ for response time and $.42$ for errors, both highly significant. These outcomes clearly suggest that a reflection-impulsivity dimension has emerged in girls at least a year prior to its appearance in boys. The contradiction between these data and the within-age correlations between KRISP response time and error scores does not lend itself to any apparent explanation.

The results of the previously described eye-movement study by McCluskey and Wright (1973) also favor females. A significant sex effect was obtained for homologous comparisons, preschool girls manifesting a higher proportion than did boys. This sex difference was in the same direction and even somewhat stronger for informative homologous comparisons. The 5-year-old females also made significantly fewer errors than their male age peers on the eye-movement task of detecting differences. Consistent with this latter finding is the evidence that females made significantly fewer errors than males on the KRISP, despite the fact that the females responded slightly faster (Wright, 1972). This strongly suggests that preschool girls may be more efficient in information processing than are preschool boys of the same age (see Wright, 1974).

These data are supportive of Maccoby's (1966) differential growth hypothesis, and they are also consistent with the sex differences on the PEFT reported in Section D of Chapter II. It should be noted, however, that Ward did not obtain results consistent with Maccoby's (1966) hypothesis regarding the disadvantage of impulsiveness for males and the advantage of impulsiveness for females in respect to level of cognitive functioning. That hypothesis, of course, depends on a mean sex difference in impulsiveness favoring males, but mean sex differences were neither substantial nor consistent in Ward's data.[10]

[10]In their recent volume, Maccoby and Jacklin (1974), on the basis of a review of

(Footnote 10 continued on page 48)

E. INFANT PRECURSORS

As indicated earlier, the reflection-impulsivity dimension represents the only cognitive style for which some effort to find infant precursors has been made. Kagan (1971) reports that boys classified as impulsive at 27 months, relative to reflectives, tend toward rapid habituation to novel stimuli at 4 months of age, a fast tempo of play at 8 months, much restless twisting during stimulus presentations at 13 months, and less time spent playing close to the mother in the latter half of a play session at 27 months. Somewhat puzzling is the use of a specially constructed EFT to assess reflection-impulsivity at 27 months, a task that does not possess obvious response-uncertainty properties and that has not yielded an inverse latency-error correlation in that age group. In their most recent communication on reflection-impulsivity, Kagan and Messer (1975), it will be recalled, considered an inverse latency-error correlation to be critical in regard to the presence of the reflection-impulsivity dimension. Overlooking this objection for the moment, it is important to note that the relationships reported by Kagan (1971) are quite weak in magnitude for boys (although statistically significant) and essentially absent in girls. In addition, EFT performance at 27 months predicted performance on MFF at 4 years of age only in the case of girls. Just what the infancy measures may be predicting in boys, then, is far from clear; they certainly are not predicting reflection-impulsivity, as that style is typically conceptualized in young children.

Kagan's (1971) conclusion in the face of the mixed outcomes just described is that "the infant's attributes obviously do not determine the impulsivity dimension, but they do exert a subtle influence on it [p. 150]." One wonders whether even this claim may not be a bit too strong. In a comparable longitudinal study in which such tempo dimensions as persistence, toy activity, vigor, and motor activity were assessed at 13, 25, and 44 months of age, Wilson and Lewis (1974) found that none of the dimensions entered into significant relationships with MFF performance at 44 months. These data are highly congruent with Ward's (1973b) finding of no relationship between practice trial times on the MIT (an obvious response-tempo measure) and MFF indexes in 4- and 5-year-olds. However, low but significant relationships between MIT practice trials and MFF latency emerge in the 6-year-olds, and similar findings are reported by Harrison and Nadelman (1972). Although tempo indices do not seem to be highly reliable or stable in Ward's (1973b) data, it is fair to say that complete independence between reflection-impulsivity and response tempo has not been established. At the same time, the overall evidence is sufficiently convincing to rule out the Kagan *et al.* (1964) hypothesis that

---

evidence indicating (in their view) no systematic sex differences in impulsiveness, have proposed that the original Maccoby (1966) model be abandoned or that a timidity- aggressiveness dimension be substituted for the earlier inhibition-impulsivity dimension.

reflection-impulsivity may, at least in part, represent an outgrowth of physio-logically based differences in response tempo. The meager evidence for linkages between reflection-impulsivity assessed by the MFF test and various indicators of response tempo is not too surprising when one considers the purported dynamics of a reflective versus impulsive style as originally delineated by Kagan and his associates. These concern anxiety over error and/or anxiety over delay. It is difficult to envision how dynamics based on considerations of anxiety can bear any relation to variations in response tempo, whether assessed in infancy or in early childhood.

F. DYNAMICS

The nature and source of the anxiety mediating a reflective or impulsive performance on the MFF remains a matter of controversy. Particularly disturb-ing is the evidence in both preschool (Ward, 1968b) and school age children (Messer, 1970; Reali & Hall, 1970) that success and failure experiences on the MFF produce a highly similar reaction in reflectives and impulsives—namely, a tendency to slow down following a failure trial and sometimes to speed up following a success trial. Whether impulsives are characterized by minimal anxiety over error or by maximal anxiety over delay in a context of low success expectancy, neither dynamic can be made to fit outcomes in which reflectives and impulsives respond similarly to success and failure contingencies.

In their recent critique of the anxiety over error formulation of reflection-impulsivity, Block et al. (1974) break with laboratory-based validation and offer instead a validation based on teachers' personality evaluations of preschool children divided into four subgroups defined by median splits on the MFF latency and error dimensions. Two of the subgroups were the slow accurates and the fast inaccurates—reflectives and impulsives, respectively, in Kagan's terms. Because these are the subjects for whom latency and error are function-ally connected in Ward's terms, there is no reason why Kagan's anxiety over error conceptualization should not be applicable to them. The sharp distinction drawn by Kagan and Messer (1975) between younger and older children can only bear on the proportion in each age group for whom the style is relevant. Given the significant negative correlation (−.33) observed between MFF latency and error in the sample studied by Block and his co-workers, the number of genuine "reflectives" and "impulsives" combined will be slightly in excess of the number of "deviant" cases—slow inaccurates and fast accurates.

A major aspect of the controversy between Block and his associates and Kagan concerns the warrant for extrapolating from the MFF and other response-uncertainty tasks to the child's spontaneous behavior in natural settings. Kagan and Messer (1975) argue against such extrapolations, quite contrary to earlier work by Kagan et al. (1964, Study 8) in which the motor activity and distracti-bility of reflective and impulsive children in a classroom setting were examined.

In currently arguing against any generalization beyond tasks containing response uncertainty, Kagan and Messer run the danger of constricting the style to the point where its practical utility is drastically curtailed. Given the current state of knowledge in the present domain, any information that bears on the implication of diverse cognitive styles for personality and behavior in "real-world" settings is surely to be welcomed. A survey of the practical educational implications of cognitive-style research (see Kogan, 1971) offers many more promissory notes than actual accomplishments. The bias in cognitive-style research has been on the side of experimental laboratory study; field-oriented work can obviously provide a corrective balance.

The sample of subjects employed in the Block *et al.* (1974) investigation included 100 children, equally divided by sex, ranging in age from 4 to 5 years, and predominantly middle SES. The California Child Q set, a 100-item modification of the adult version (Block, 1961, 1971) appropriate for preschool children, was used to obtain personality characterizations from the children's nursery-school teachers. These then were analyzed from the perspective of Q items that discriminate children fast versus slow on MFF latency and high versus low on MFF errors. In addition, Q items relevant to significant latency-error interactions were noted. This entailed a search for Q items discriminating between all possible pairs of the 2×2 matrix generated by median splits on latency and errors. It need hardly be stated that a massive number of comparisons are involved in the foregoing analyses, and it is simply impossible in this chapter to convey the richness and subtlety of the personality differences linked to variations in MFF performance. At best, we can merely select some of the more salient outcomes, particularly those that seem most crucially related to prior conceptualizations of reflection-impulsivity dynamics.

Where overall effects are concerned, only two Q items were related significantly to variation in MFF latency, whereas 32 Q items were significantly associated with variation in MFF errors. An additional 18 Q items achieved significance by virtue of the interaction between latency and error. It is quite clear, then, that MFF latency as such has much weaker implications for observed behaviors in the school context than does the MFF error component taken by itself. At the same time, latency had a considerable impact on Q-item differences through interaction with the dimension of error.

One aspect of the data collected by Block and his co-workers is cause for some concern. Whereas intelligence (WPPSI full scale IQ) was relatively independent of MFF latency ($r = .14$), the former was significantly associated with MFF error scores ($r = -.39$). Because no IQ controls were incorporated into the data analysis, some of the variance shared by MFF errors and the assorted Q items must also be IQ variance. It is entirely legitimate to argue, of course, that errors on MFF have causal priority, the process that elevates error level being partially responsible for depressed IQ levels. Nevertheless, as a first attempt to link reflection-impulsivity to the broad domain of personality, it can only be regretted that the MFF error score has not been purified by removal of IQ covariance before relationships with personality characteristics were delineated. The failure to do so implies that some of the MFF-personality associations to be described would cease to be significant, if an IQ control were applied. Unfortunately, we do not know which of the numerous relationships reported would survive such an analysis and which would not.[11]

On the basis of the Q items differentiating children who made few as opposed to many errors on the MFF, Block et al. (1974) described the two groups as follows:

The Accurates are identified as comparatively competent, resourceful, empathic, interpersonally attractive children—they are more socially perceptive, brighter, more reasonable, more approachable individuals. The Inaccurates, on the other hand, appear to be relatively vulnerable, poorly defended, demanding, overly sensitive and brittle children—they are more lacking in self-confidence, more likely to feel discriminated against, tend to be more rigid, and are less happy [p. 626].

Those authors believe that the foregoing contrast is highly consistent with the ego-resiliency concept (Block, 1965; Block & Block, 1973), for the fundamental differences between the accurates and inaccurates concerns the ability to make successful adaptations to environmental demands. It should be noted, congruent with previous observations, that accurate and inaccurate groups also differed significantly in IQ. Block and associates suggest that IQ, as "usually and narrowly conceived" could not easily accommodate the diversity of behaviors and personality dispositions distinguishing the accurate versus inaccurate groups. An obvious rejoinder is that, no matter how narrowly IQ may be conceived, it is necessarily broader than an MFF error score. Such polemic could easily be set aside, of course, by the kind of statistical analysis recommended— namely, controlling for IQ in the search for Q items that differentiate high and low MFF-error groups.

For the Blocks and their associates, two central dimensions in the personality domain—ego resiliency (previously cited) and ego control—were considered to be particularly relevant in the present context. The latter is bipolar with overcontrol at one pole and undercontrol at the other (see Block, 1965; Block & Block, 1973). Both of these can be adaptive or maladaptive depending on the intrinsic task requirements or demand quality of the situation. The ego-control dimension articulates with Kagan's conceptualization of reflection-impulsivity, for the cautious versus risklike behaviors typical of a highly reflective versus a highly impulsive performance on the MFF at least carries the connotation of

[11]There is a broader issue here that cannot be ignored. Does IQ always deserve the status of a control variable in partial correlational analysis? As indicated earlier, there is an obvious need to apply analytic models to cognitive style-IQ relationships that attempt to derive causal explanations from nonexperimental longitudinal data. If it should be shown that IQ is more likely to be an outcome than a cause, the automatic assignment of IQ to the status of a necessary control variable could be seriously questioned.

overcontrol versus undercontrol, respectively. At the same time, of course, the ego-resiliency concept is relevant because reflectivity is linked to adaptive and impulsivity to madadaptive behaviors.

Do the personality characteristics associated with the four quadrants of the error-latency matrix in the data of Block and his associates fit the dynamics of reflection-impulsivity as presently conceived? The fit appears reasonably good for the slow accurates (reflectives). They are the children scoring lowest among the four quadrants on the "undercontrol index," and the traits attributed to them are suggestive of some caution, constraint, and docility, although in a context of interpersonal maturity, competence, and diligence. The degree of fit for the fast inaccurates (the impulsives in Kagan's classification) depends on which of the alternative conceptualizations of impulsivity dynamics is selected. If the more recent view (Kagan & Kogan, 1970) of impulsivity as representing "minimal anxiety over error" is accepted, the fit with the personality characterization offered by Block and his associates is not close. Such traits as anxious, vulnerable, tense, cautious, and self-doubting are applied to the fast inaccurate children. On this basis, Block and his associates reject the foregoing view of impulsivity-dynamics offered by Kagan and offer an alternative view deriving from research published 20 years ago by Block and Petersen (1955) and Smock (1955).

This alternative view maintains that the fast and inaccurate responder experiences intense anxiety in an unfamiliar testing situation. Lacking a well-learned response to the MFF, the fast inaccurate child is presumed to seize on a possible answer prematurely, because such a response serves the anxiety-reducing function of bringing closure to the task and temporarily removing him from the situation.

In all fairness to Kagan, it should be noted that a similar interpretation to the foregoing had been advanced approximately 10 years ago in the monograph that first introduced the reflection-impulsivity construct (Kagan et al., 1964). At that time, Kagan and his associates suggested that impulsivity might derive from the child's anxiety about the testing situation and his expectancies of failure, both contributing to an inability to tolerate delay in the service of accurate response selection. It is not entirely clear as to why Kagan has moved away from the foregoing interpretation in favor of a position that attributes minimal anxiety to the impulsive child (Kagan & Kogan, 1970). In their rejoinder to Block et al. (1974), Kagan and Messer (1975) imply that there is no basic contradiction in the alternative interpretations, for different sources of anxiety are presumed to be relevant to reflectives and impulsives. According to the latter authors, "it is useful to distinguish between anxiety over one's basic ability to perform a task, which can lead to an impulsive performance, and anxiety over making an error on a task one believes one can solve [p. 247]." This is a meaningful distinction, to be sure, but one that respresents an inference from MFF performance rather than one that is operationally defined independently of MFF error and latency scores.

Block and his co-workers have also examined the personality characteristics associated with slow inaccurate and fast accurate responding on the MFF. Qualities suggestive of enthusiasm, self-confidence, independence, and resourcefulness are attributed to fast accurates by their teachers. The fast accurates, in sum, appear to be a psychologically robust group, but one should not forget that they are, comparatively speaking, a highly intelligent group.

At the opposite extreme, one finds the slow inaccurates. These children tend to be described as uninhibited, unable to delay gratification, egocentric, and "acting out." These qualities strongly suggest impulsiveness and, in fact, the slow inaccurates do yield the highest mean score on the Blocks' index of undercontrol. Those authors assert, on the basis of the foregoing findings, that impulsiveness (as a general personality characteristic) does not have to be associated with an impulsive mode of responding (fast latencies) on the MFF. Kagan and Messer (1975) do not find these data particularly disturbing on the grounds that there never has been any intent to generalize from an impulsive mode of responding on tasks distinguished by response uncertainty to impulsiveness as a trait. In a subsequent reply, however, Block et al. (1975) have noted instances where Kagan has extrapolated from MFF performance to more generalized behaviors.

G. METHODOLOGICAL ALTERNATIVES

As research on the reflection-impulsivity construct has proceeded, the level of dissatisfaction with its manner of measurement has steadily increased. The typical assessment of the construct, as discussed earlier, has been based on simultaneous median splits along the latency and error dimensions. Of the four resultant quadrants, the two that reflect the inverse correlation between latencies and errors—slow accurates and fast inaccurates—have been designated reflectives and impulsives, respectively. Such a classification system forces the exclusion of subjects in the off-diagonal cells—the fast accurates and slow inaccurates—and hence necessarily implies the discarding of potentially useful information. Research by Ault, et al. (1972) and Block et al. (1974) (discussed earlier in Section III. F) has in fact shown rather strikingly how the inclusion of these oft-neglected subjects in the study design helps to clarify the underlying processes at work within the framework of response-uncertainty tasks.

Although the four-way classification described represents an obvious improvement over the original two-way split, difficulties still remain. The adequacy of any classification scheme based on the subdivision of a continuous distribution (whether dichotomized at the median or cut more finely) depends on the statistical reliability of the measure. Whereas latency appears to generate very substantial internal-consistency reliabilities, MFF error scores have yielded rather modest coefficient alphas ranging from the low 30s to the low 60s (Ault, Mitchell, & Hartman, 1976 Block et al., 1974). Error reliabilities in that range must necessarily imply that there is a strong chance factor at work when median splits are employed. Some children located within a fairly broad band around the median might conceivably be designated as reflectives one day but reclassified as slow inaccurates the following week on a readministration of the MFF. Similarly, other children classified initially as impulsive might subsequently be reassigned to the fast accurate cell. One solution to this problem of unreliability is the exclusive use of extreme groups. Apart from the practical disadvantage of this "solution" (large samples would be required), the discarding of subjects would essentially reintroduce the basic shortcoming of the original two-way classification.

These problems have generally not deterred investigators from using two-way or four-way splits on latency and error scores as independent variables in simple *t* tests and analysis of variance designs. As Ault *et al.* (1976) have pointed out, this practice is ill conceived in at least two respects. First, artificial dichotomization always implies a loss of considerable variance and hence weakens statistical power. This carries the implication that the reflection-impulsivity literature may suffer from an underestimation of the magnitude of its relations with other variables. Second, the use of correlated dimensions (latency and error) as independent variables violates analysis of variance assumptions. Such designs can only result in confounded main and interaction effects.

There is an obvious solution to the foregoing difficulties, and that is to dispense with dichotomization and classification entirely. As Ault *et al.* (1976) have noted, multiple regression (see Kerlinger & Pedhazur, 1973) is ideally suited for the analysis of the kind of data generated by MFF and similar tasks. The technique treats latency and error as continuous variables and hence does not entail the squandering of information inherent to dichotomization. Furthermore, the technique is designed to deal with correlated independent variables. The inverse correlation between latency and error scores is put to use in estimating the effects of each in respect to the dependent variable of interest.

A further gain that results from the retention of latencies and errors as continuous variables is the facilitation of norm development. So long as investigators employ median splits tied to specific samples, there is no guarantee (even with chronological age held constant) that children from different samples will be classified identically despite similar latency and error scores. Variation in classification seriously compromises the generalizability of findings from sample to sample. Where classification is avoided, means and standard deviations for response times and errors provide a simple and straightforward comparative yardstick.

The superiority of the multiple-regression procedure for the analysis of MFF data is so highly compelling that one can only puzzle at the fact that there is not as yet a single study in the published literature that has used the technique.[12] Conceivably, the labeling of a construct (particularly if value laden) prompts

---

[12] I have recently learned of such a study currently in press (Haskins & McKinney, 1976).

psychologists toward conceptualizations that are categorical rather than dimensional. It appears to be psychologically easier to think in terms of reflective and impulsive children as opposed to a normally distributed continuum on which children are located. Analytic techniques then seem to follow that preserve the imposed categorization.

Although multiple-regression techniques can readily handle the observed inverse correlation between response time and errors, this does not necessarily imply that those raw scores are the only or even the best way to represent performance on such response-uncertainty tasks as MFF or KRISP. A novel alternative approach has been recently offered by Wright (1974). That author maintains that the reflection-impulsivity construct includes both stylistic and ability variance. Accordingly, Wright suggests that MFF or KRISP performance be simultaneously classified along the two orthogonal dimensions of "impulsivity" (style) and "cognitive efficiency" (ability). Recently, Salkind (1975) has provided scoring formulas for these separate dimensions based on standard score combinations of latencies and error.[13] Although both represent continuous dimensions, they can be dichotomized at the median to yield a four-way classification.

Although Salkind's research is based on elementary-school children (second and third graders), the scoring formulas are equally applicable to preschoolers and hence it is of interest to compare his I versus E classification outcomes with the traditional four-way latency-error classification. All of the children classified as reflective or impulsive by the usual procedure retained that classification with the I-score formula (low versus high I score, respectively). Traditional slow inaccurates split 73% (high I score) versus 27% (low I score). The fast accurate group divided more evenly, 47% receiving a low I score and 53% receiving a high I score. In respect to the E score, all of the children traditionally designated as fast accurates and slow inaccurates were reclassified as efficient and inefficient, respectively. The children customarily designated as reflectives and impulsives were about equally likely to be assigned to the efficient and inefficient quadrants. It is evident that the style versus efficiency distinction does not do violence to the typical classification based on error and latency scores.

In Wright's (1974) terms, a major advantage of the new classification system is the opportunity it offers of removing the pervasive value bias in the

[13] The formula for impulsivity (I score) is as follows:

$$I_i = (z_{ei} - z_{li})/2$$

where I is the impulsivity score for the ith individual, z_{ei} is the standard score for the ith individual's MFF total errors, and z_{li} is the standard score for the ith individual's MFF mean latency. The formula for cognitive efficiency (E score) is as follows:

$$E_i = (z_{ci} + z_{li})/2$$

where E_i = efficiency score for the ith individual. Note that a negative E score indicates efficient performance.

reflection-impulsivity literature. The extraction of a pure stylistic dimension (an unprecedented shift from a Type I to a Type III cognitive style) from MFF or KRISP performance is viewed as a means toward a more value-balanced perspective in which an impulsive style would be advantageous and a reflective style disadvantageous in certain contexts or circumstances.[14] It is not clear, however, how the value issue can be entirely dismissed when a cognitive efficiency dimension is required to account fully for variation in MFF performance.

Salkind's work represents the only empirical examination of I- and E-score correlates. In a sample of 93 elementary-school children, scores derived from the Primary Mental Abilities (PMA) test (Thurstone & Thurstone, 1963) were found to correlate negatively and significantly with the E score. Consistent with expectations, the more efficient children exceeded their less efficient peers on verbal meaning, spatial relations, number facility, and perceptual speed. At the same time, however, the I score was also negatively related to performance on the PMA subtests. The correlations, although consistently smaller ($-.18$ to $-.25$) than those obtained with the E score ($-.21$ to $-.44$), were nevertheless statistically significant. Although such findings may appear to run counter to Wright's views about the value-free quality of the stylistic I score, it is not unreasonable to assume that the cognitive advantages of impulsivity are least likely to find expression on standardized intellective tests. The advantages that accrue to an impulsive style very probably lie in the domains of the imaginative and the creative. Although Ward (1968a) did not find a significant relation between the traditional reflection-impulsivity assessment and scores on the Wallach and Kogan (1965) divergent-thinking tasks, it would be of considerable interest to reexamine the impulsivity-creativity relationship in young children using the I-score method just described.

Further contributing to the construct validity of the style-efficiency classification is Salkind's evidence that the age of the child bears no relation to the stylistic I score, whereas age is significantly associated with the E score ($r = -.29$). Older children are more efficient but not necessarily less impulsive. These findings strengthen the view that variance in the I score has more to do with individual style than with developmental level as such. It will be recalled that this issue formed the basis of the Achenbach and Weisz (1975) critique. The matter is far from definitively settled, however, for Salkind's subjects had reached the age (7 to 8 years) where developmental change is less rapid than is the case in the preschool years. Thus far, the style-efficiency model initially

---

[14]Wright has suggested that impulsive children are likely to be imaginative and creative children. This hypothesis has not been confirmed, however. Ward (1968a) failed to find a relationship between MFF performance and creative ability on the Wallach-Kogan tasks. More recently, Fuqua, Bartsch, and Phye (1975) observed that reflective preschoolers performed better than their impulsive peers on one of Torrance's figural tests.

formulated by Wright (1974) and substantially developed by Salkind (1975) has not yet been applied to preschool children.

Although the evidence is presently quite limited in scope, its overall pattern favors the view that classifying subjects in terms of I and E scores represents an improvement over the traditional latency vs error classification. Whereas the latter is distinguished by a high degree of overlapping variance, the I- vs E-score distinction offers dimensions that seem to be more independent. Clearly needed is further evidence testifying to the claim that a style vs capacity contrast is reflected by the two scores. The possibility of obtaining stylistic and ability components from the same performance has enormous appeal on conceptual grounds, but further construct validation research is necessary before this promising analytic model can be considered the definitive way to score the MFF, KRISP, and other similar tasks.

One final question must be asked. If the analytic complexities introduced by virtue of the negative correlation between latency and error are readily handled within the framework of the multiple-regression model, is there any justification for further development of the Wright-Salkind approach? It should be first pointed out that the I and E scores are also continuous variables that lend themselves to multiple-regression analysis. The question, therefore, cannot obviously be resolved on statistical grounds alone. The latency versus error distinction has the advantage of staying close to the raw data. The I- versus E-score distinction entails more complicated scoring but is conceptually more compelling. No doubt, the field will soon witness comparative tests of the two scoring methods and, in due course, one or the other will very probably become standard operating procedure.

H.   CONCLUSIONS AND IMPLICATIONS

It is apparent from the foregoing extended treatment of the reflection-impulsivity construct that the field is in a state of ferment. There is no doubt that efforts to extend that cognitive style downward to the preschool years and infancy have opened up a range of new and controversial issues. The major controversy has concerned the Kagan and Block research groups, a controversy that has been relatively healthy for the field in the sense of clarifying certain issues and posing others in need of further investigation. The recent research by Ward and by Wright also deserves commendation for the manner in which they have highlighted crucial and previously neglected aspects of the problem. Let us then take stock of where matters stand in respect to reflection-impulsivity in preschool children and possible precursors in infancy.

First, there can be no doubt that the dynamics of an impulsive performance on the MFF have been clarified. The hypothesis that minimal anxiety over error characterizes the impulsive child has not fared well under empirical examination.

The hypothesis that different types of anxiety characterize reflectives and impulsives—anxiety over error versus anxiety over task competence—appears to be more viable.[15]

Second, it has been demonstrated that the information-processing styles and skills of the preschool child extend beyond the strictly cognitive domain to incorporate aspects of personality and social behavior.

Third, the genuinely developmental aspects of the reflection-impulsivity construct have been finally brought to the fore. It is now clear that there is some developmental point (possibly varying with the sex and SES of the child) below which it is no longer meaningful to speak of a reflective versus impulsive style even though latency and errors are readily measurable.

When median splits on latency and errors are employed to divide children into four subgroups—reflectives, impulsives, fast accurates, and slow inaccurates—the salient developmental issue concerns the direction of movement from one subgroup to another. In Ward's terms, the developmental trend is away from independent response tempo (latency) and ability (error) determinants of MFF performance toward a task-oriented, self-regulated, functionally connected linkage between latency and error. By this criterion, one may infer that both reflectives and impulsives are developmentally more mature than their off-diagonal peers, because both of the former groups must contribute to the latency-error inverse relation. The difficulty with such a positon is that, whereas it may account for the slow inaccurates (whose qualities in the research of Block and his co-workers do suggest developmental immaturity), the qualities of the fast accurate children point to an advanced rather than a lagging developmental course.

In conclusion, consider the matter of infant precursors. As we have seen, reflection-impulsivity represents the only cognitive style for which longitudinal data extending to infancy exists. The data, however, have been disappointing, as relationships between tempo indices in infancy and reflection-impulsivity scores in the preschool years have turned out to be negligible or inconsistent. In my view, it would be worth the effort to examine the data from a different analytic perspective. As Ward has shown, a low to moderate negative correlation between latency and error does not imply a weak association for all subjects but indicates the absence of an association for some children and a strong association for

---

[15]Further complicating the issue are the studies (e.g., Messer, 1970) indicating that the experimental enhancement of anxiety over error increases the latencies and reduces the error rates of impulsive children. At first blush, these results appear to suggest that impulsives simply have less anxiety over error than do reflectives. It is equally if not more likely, however, that the feedback provided by the experimenter mitigates the anxiety over task competence experienced by the impulsive (fast inaccurate) child. As Block et al. (1974) suggest, "lowering of the error rates of Fast/Inaccurates in modification studies. . . may be due to the ambiguity reducing effects of the explicit structure provided to these structure-requiring and structure-seeking children [p. 630]."

others. A straightforward correlational analysis conceals the foregoing distinction. If a negligible latency-error connection implies the presence of response tempo and ability variance in preschoolers, linkages with tempo and cognitive indicators in infancy should be stronger than in the case where latency and error have been drawn into a functional relation on response-uncertainty tasks. Before the search for infant precursors in the present domain is abandoned, the type of moderator analysis suggested clearly deserves a trial.

IV

Breadth of Categorization

A. GENERAL BACKGROUND

When a person is made aware of the central-tendency value or is given a focal exemplar of a particular category, wide individual variation has been observed in the setting of boundary limitations for that category. Some individuals are relatively narrow in the sense of rejecting instances that, in their subjective opinion, stray too far from the central or focal value; others are able to accommodate a broader range of instances by subjectively setting category boundaries a considerable distance from the central tendency or focal exemplar.

A wide variety of tasks—quantitative, geometric, and verbal—have been employed to assess category breadth in older children, adolescents, and adults (see Kogan, 1971). In the quantitative domain, the Pettigrew (1958) instrument offers a central-tendency value for a variety of categories (for example, annual rainfall, width of windows, length of whales), and the subject is required to choose the upper and lower boundaries for the category from among the multiple-choice options provided. Wallach and Caron (1959) used a geometric concept-attainment task in which children learned that "poggles" represented a class of figures with a particular angle. Subsequently, the children were shown a series of figures varying only in acuteness of angle, with the requirement that they distinguish members of the series on the basis of whether or not they belonged to the "poggle" class. Finally, in the verbal area, Fillenbaum (1959) constructed a word-synonym task in which subjects had to check all words in a set of 10 alternatives that could be substituted for a key word in a sentence without an essential alteration in meaning. Despite the diverse content represented by the foregoing tasks, all share the common property of providing an average or focal value and requiring the subject to establish the outer limits of the category in question. Reasonable generality across content domains in preferred breadth versus narrowness has been observed for the kinds of "bandwidth" tasks described. Although these tasks have been administered to samples of children, systematic studies directed to the issue of developmental change in "bandwidth" preferences over the childhood period or later have only recently begun to appear (see Mervis, Catlin, & Rosch, 1975).[1]

Studies of "category breadth" have not been confined to tasks of the "bandwidth" type. Object-sorting tasks (e.g., Gardner, 1953) also offer the opportunity to observe breadth of categorization. In this type of procedure, the subject is typically presented with an array of common objects (or pictures of such objects) and is requested to group the objects into the "most comfortable" number of categories. Individuals vary in the number and size of groupings formed. Some prefer to construct a few groups with a fairly large number of exemplars per group; others form more groups with a rather small number of instances contained in each. This contrast has been characterized as broad versus narrow "equivalence range" by Gardner (1953) and subsequently as low versus high conceptual differentiation, respectively, by Gardner and Schoen (1962). Object-sorting tasks also tend to generate ungrouped singles to a varying degree across subjects. Messick and Kogan (1963) have employed the term "compartmentalization" to refer to the number of miscellaneous objects left ungrouped. Compartmentalization appears to be independent of the number of groupings containing two or more instances.

As in the case of "bandwidth" tasks, object-sorting procedures generate interindividual consistency across content domains. For example, Gardner and Schoen (1962) obtained significant levels of generality for objects, photos, and behavior statements. Similar findings are reported by Glixman (1965), who employed objects, self-referent statements, and attitudinal items. Preference for a large, intermediate, or small number of groupings appears to be consistent across a diverse set of domains.

Developmental data (cross-sectional) from kindegarten through adulthood have been reported for a variety of sorting tasks (Annett, 1959; Gardner & Moriarty, 1968; Goldman & Levine, 1963; Reichard, Schneider, & Rapaport, 1944; Sigel, 1953). The general trend in these data is toward increasing breadth

[1] It should be noted that the general thrust of this research (e.g., Heider, 1971, 1972; Rosch, 1973, 1974) has concerned the nature and development of the focal areas of categories (rather than boundaries), particularly in the domain of colors. The Mervis *et al.* (1975) paper represents the first systematic comparison of focal and boundary areas of color categories from a developmental perspective. Of particular interest is the evidence from that study indicating that kindergarten children, third graders, and adults do not differ in choice of chips representing the foci of color categories. The interindividual variance of such judgments decreases progressively with age, however. This suggests that choice of the focal member of a category (as well as boundary choices) could be explored from an individual-difference perspective in young children.

of categorization as the age of the subject increases. Kogan (1971) has suggested that these age trends are consistent with other developmental evidence (e.g., Bruner, Olver, & Greenfield, 1966; Vygotsky, 1962) pointing to shifts away from an emphasis on perceptual differences toward conceptually based abstraction and synthesis.

Although a dimension of breadth versus narrowness is common to bandwidth and object-sorting procedures, a consistent strategy across the two types of tasks has not been demonstrated across all of the relevant studies (see Kogan, 1971). A reasonable hypothesis, one that has not yet been explicity confirmed, is that the strength of the relationship between the two classes of categorizing at issue increases as the similarity in content domain increases. Reasons can be advanced, however, as to why a strong relationship should not be anticipated. Where the sorting task is completely open in format, subjects are necessarily forced to search for the appropriate categories to which exemplars can be assigned. In the case of bandwidth tasks, an instance rejected for category membership is assigned to limbo; in the object-sorting procedure, an instance deemed inappropriate for one category may find a home in another.

Not all of the object-sorting procedures described in the literature make use of the completely open format employed by Gardner (1953). Often, the investigator (e.g., Sigel, 1972) offers exemplars of possible categories to the subject whose task is to select the available objects in the array that can be grouped with each of the exemplars provided. Such a procedure necessarily eliminates individual variation in the number of possible groupings formed; only the number of instances per exemplar is of interest. The resemblance to the bandwidth type of task has become closer, and one might well anticipate that the empirical linkage would be stronger. Regrettably, evidence relevant to the issue is lacking. Despite the enhanced similarity, however, it should be noted that an important difference remains. In the bandwidth case, the category is totally unambiguous and the judgment concerns its quantitative extent; in "constrained" object sorting, subjects may continue to vary in the kind of category formed, and this variation can conceivably influence the breadth of the category.

In comparing breadth of categorization with the cognitive styles discussed in Chapters II and III, it is important to note how value considerations have declined somewhat in importance in the present case. Although several investigators have observed an increase in category breadth with age, such outcomes appear to be confined to object-sorting tasks. Consistent age trends have not been reported in the case of bandwidth tasks (see Mervis et al., 1975). Furthermore, it may be the link between category breadth and higher-level abstraction in the sorting paradigm that produces the observed age trend rather than breadth as such.

For children of preschool age, breadth of categorization may operate independently of abstraction and superordination. The overall consistency and accuracy of performance may assume greater prominence. It is possible, of course, to impose a quality criterion in the object-sorting procedure in the sense of rating the appropriateness and adequacy of the groupings that are formed. Kennedy and Kates (1964) for example, have done so in the case of 12-year-olds and have found that the more poorly adjusted and less intelligent children manifest relatively more inaccuracies in their sorting behavior. No attempt was made, however, to explore the relationship between breadth and accuracy. As we shall presently see, level of accuracy or consistency is a critical feature of the preschooler's performance on tasks of category breadth.

B.   ASSESSMENT IN PRESCHOOL CHILDREN

A number of studies have been published in which preschool and older children have been compared on various indices of categorization breadth. There is also research currently in progress on differences within the preschool period, some of it based on children as young as 18 months of age. Most of the foregoing research has had a developmental rather than an individual-differences focus. Only the Block and Block (1973) project has concentrated on individual differences in breadth of categorization at the preschool level. In the subsequent paragraphs, the developmental perspective is discussed first, followed by the work on individual variation among preschoolers in breadth and accuracy (or consistency) of categorization.

1.   Developmental Mean Differences
Spanning Preschool and Later Age Periods

One group of investigators (Saltz, 1971; Saltz & Sigel, 1967; Saltz, Soller, & Sigel, 1972) has strongly endorsed the view that development entails a shift from narrowness to breadth of categorization. As expressed by Saltz et al. (1972), "conceptual development is most strongly characterized by a shift away from overdiscrimination and toward integration rather than a shift away from overgeneralization and toward differentiation [p. 1202]." It should be noted that the latter position was initially formulated by Gibson and Gibson (1955) and subsequently expanded by Gibson (1969).

Let us consider the research of Saltz and his colleagues in some detail. The first of these (Saltz & Sigel, 1967) did not use children younger than 6 years of age, but the study nevertheless deserves consideration here for the sake of continuity with the later work. In that study, the stimulus materials consisted of photographs of boys faces. Several photos were taken of each boy showing different facial expressions and head positions. Subjects—6-year-olds, 9-year-olds, and adults—were shown a standard photo of a particular boy's face and had to specify whether three successively presented variants were of the same or a different boy. The measure of category breadth in the present context is the number of variants accepted as the same boy represented by the standard. Accuracy is assessed on the basis of whether the subjects' judgments of "same" or "different" actually corresponded to matching (same boy) or nonmatching (different boy) photos, respectively.

The outcomes of the Saltz-Sigel investigation showed a preponderance of overdiscrimination errors in the 6-year-olds and of overgeneralization errors in the adults. The youngest subjects, in other words, exhibited quite narrow categorization, frequently rejecting as "different" photos that were actually of the same boy. The adult subjects, by contrast, showed broad categorization tendencies in the sense of accepting two photos of different boys as representative of the same boy. It is not surprising to find that the overgeneralization tendency in the adults was less strong than the overdiscrimination tendency in the children. As a result, adults exhibited better overall accuracy. However, there was a special subset of items—where the standard and the instance looked highly similar, although they were actually different—where 6-year-olds made fewer errors than adults. Of course, this represented a fortuitous byproduct of young children's disposition toward narrow categorizing in the present experimental context.

The subsequent study by Saltz et al. (1972) used kindergarten, third-, and sixth-grade children, 12 boys and 12 girls at each grade level. The procedure consisted of the presentation of concept labels (food, animal, transportation, clothes, toy, furniture) to the child, who then had to specify which instances (in the form of colored pictures of objects, 72 in all) were appropriate to the label. Highly significant effects were obtained in the direction of fewer pictures assigned to concept labels on the part of the youngest (kindergarten) children. Differences between the third and sixth graders were negligible. The pattern of the differences did not change when the instances were divided into "core" and "noncore" items (chosen by more or less than 75% of the children as an instance of a particular concept).

Saltz and his associates concluded that kindergarten-age children, relative to their older peers, use concept names in a more fragmented, narrow, and inappropriately delimiting fashion. Development is presumed to have the effect of integrating the narrow fragments into a broader and more veridical concept. The observed narrowness of the youngest children is attributed to their dependence on perceptual attributes in categorizing instances. Saltz and his coworkers cite the example of a picture of a cow, which bears no perceptual similarity to food and hence was assigned to the food category less frequently by younger than by older children. At the same time, however, those authors refer to another item—a picture of a stuffed animal—which is more likely to be assigned to the animal category by younger than by older children. Here then is an indication of the overgeneralization of the younger child consistent with the Gibson and Gibson (1955) position. Saltz and his associates rightfully claim on the basis of their data that overgeneralization is less typical of the youngest children than is overdiscrimination. The indication that both are present, however, opens the possibility that either narrowness or breadth can be enhanced depending on the concept labels and pictorial instances chosen.

In the original Gibson and Gibson (1955) research, adults, older children (8—11 years), and younger children (6—8 years) were provided with a set of cards containing a standard "scribble" and a set of variants; the subjects' task required the identification of those cards identical to the standard.[2] Striking age differences were obtained in the direction of greater acceptance of non-identical variants with decreasing age of the subject.

Vurpillot (1968) obtained comparable results in four groups of children averaging approximately 4, 5, 7, and 9 years of age. The stimulus materials consisted of pictures of houses presented in pairs with each house containing six identifiable components. Some of the pairs were identical and the others varied in their degree of difference (one, three, or five components). The child had to specify whether the various pairs were the same or different. The results were quite clear-cut: except for the children in the oldest group (who manifested almost perfect accuracy), errors were considerably more likely on the different pairs than on the identical pairs. It is apparent that the younger children did not scan the stimulus pair thoroughly and hence were likely to attribute a similarity (overgeneralization) when it was not warranted. If the pair happened to be identical, of course, accuracy was assured.

How can one account for the stiking contrast between the research of the Gibsons and of Vurpillot, on the one hand, and of Saltz and Sigel (1967), on the other? It will be recalled that the youngest children in the latter experiment were considerably more disposed toward the attribution of an unwarranted difference (overdiscrimination and category narrowness) than an unwarranted similarity (overgeneralization and category breadth). Again, the stimulus materials employed seem to be crucial. The "scribbles" and "houses" described above require active scanning of distinctive features for a difference to be noticed and, as we have seen, younger children are less able or willing to make the systematic effort required. The faces employed by Saltz and Sigel, in contrast, are immediately recognizable as "different" even when they are of the same boy from various angles. It is the recognition of identity (same boy) in the context of genuine stimulus difference that demands a more active perceptual comparison. Not surprisingly, older subjects are more likely to manifest the latter tendency with the natural consequence of occasional overgeneralization errors. In sum, breadth versus narrowness of categorization can proceed in either direction with age depending on the class of stimuli at issue. Where differences are immediately recognizable (as in the case of faces or other Gestalts), narrowness (overdiscrimination) is likely to precede breadth (overgeneralization)

---

[2]Unlike the MFF task, where the standard and variants are presented simultaneously, the Gibsons expose the standard and the set of variants successively. The former exludes the memory component, whereas the latter requires the match of a memory image with current stimulation.

over the course of development. Where the apprehension of differences requires active visual scanning, the developmental trend is likely to proceed in the opposite direction, that is, from breadth (overgeneralization) to narrowness (overdiscrimination). It should be understood, of course, that developmental shifts along a broad versus narrow dimension do not necessarily imply the presence of judgmental error. Overdiscrimination and overgeneralization merely refer to the kinds of errors likely to be made at the narrow and broad extremes, respectively, of the categorization style dimension.

The methodological considerations described above do not apply to the Saltz *et al.* (1972) research on the development of natural language concepts, and hence it is fair to inquire whether one can unequivocally accept the conclusions of that research in respect to the developmental shift from narrow, fragmented concepts to broad, integrated concepts. Serious questions about the foregoing research are raised in a partial replication recently published by Neimark (1974). That author used the "food" and "clothing" classes from Saltz *et al.* (1972) and added the classes of "things to eat" and "things to wear." The subjects were second and sixth graders and college students. Whereas no difference was found for the number of items included in the "food" and "things to eat" categories, a significant difference distinguished the "clothes" and "things to wear" categories. Second graders included approximately the same number of items in each, but sixth graders and college students actually decreased the number of items encompassed by the "clothing" relative to the "things to wear" class. The older subjects, in other words, fractionated "things to wear" into clothing and accessories, whereas the youngest subjects made no such differentiation.

The direction of the difference reported by Neimark (1974)—greater breadth in the younger subjects—is quite the opposite of what Saltz and co-workers would have predicted. It should also be noted that three of the four categories employed by Neimark yielded a highly comparable number of items included for the three age groups. This last finding is not particularly damaging to the position espoused by Saltz and his associates, however, because the latter's research included a sample of kindergarten children. These are the children whose performance differed from the third and sixth graders in the Saltz *et al.* (1972) study. Neimark's youngest group was in the second grade, a point where the major developmental transition may have already taken place. Nevertheless, the mere fact that one of the four concept classes in the Neimark research manifested a broad to narrow shift forces the conclusion that developmental trends in respect to breadth versus narrowness of categorization may well depend on the class labels and the instances provided for categorization.

More is at issue, however, than the particular stimulus materials employed. There is the matter of the character of the task itself. In a recent provocative study, Katherine Nelson (1974a) proposes that the alleged category narrowness typical of early childhood may actually reflect the kinds of assessment procedures employed. Using a semantic memory task in which the child was simply requested to recall instances of a series of well-known categories (for example, animals, clothes, colors, flowers, fruit), Nelson observed little difference between 5- and 8-year-olds in the setting of boundaries for the diverse categories represented in the study. There was no indication in the data that young children's categories were more constricted. Instead, there was a tendency in both age groups to generate "marginal" as well as "core" instances, the former representing an obvious effort to extend the boundaries of the category beyond its customary limits. Within the established boundaries of the category, the older children produced more instances. However, this superiority seems to reflect the fact that the older child's categories were more hierarchal and articulated than the younger child's. The observed age difference had little connection to the breadth of the category. To the degree, however, that "marginal" instances decrease at later ages, it should be safe to presume that categories become more narrow with increasing age.

The foregoing findings naturally lead to the question of the basis for the commonly accepted generalization that categories become broader as the age of the child increases. Nelson offers two reasons for the striking discrepancies between her research and work published previously. First, she asserts that experimenter demand characteristics are not so salient in the context of free recall. Unfortunately, it is not immediately clear why a straightforward object-sorting task should possess more demand characteristics than does a task of free recall. The second reason offered by Nelson is considerably more solid. She maintains that the use of objects or pictorial representations with young children results in an artificial narrowing of concepts because of the sensitivity to perceptual differences typical of such subjects.

Although Nelson deserves much credit for showing that the developmental course is just as likely to proceed from broad to narrow categorizing as in the opposite direction, it is not possible to claim that she is in any sense more correct than her predecessors. Instead, the contrast merely serves to emphasize the great relevance of the task and the materials employed in forming inferences about the breadth of categorization domain. Indeed, Mervis *et al.* (1975) have demonstrated that the developmental course for category boundary judgments varies for different dimensions within the same task. Twenty kindergarten children, 20 third graders, and 20 adults were shown 320 chromatic chips mounted on a board so that the rows reflected variation in hue and the columns reflected variation in brightness. Subjects were read a list of 11 color names and requested to choose all of the chips to which the name could be applied. For the brightness dimension, the kindergarten and third grade group did not differ, but adults differed significantly in the direction of greater breadth (accepting more brightness levels). In respect to the hue dimension, in contrast, a significant progressive decrease in breadth was observed as subject age increased. In a final study based only on third graders and adults, hue and brightness were held constant and saturation varied. Again, adults manifested greater breadth (that is, accepted chips with lower saturation within the color category boundaries). A final finding worthy of note is the much stronger tendency of kindergarten children (relative to third graders and adults) to accept the same chip as being within the boundaries of more than one color. This finding points to a possible inverse relation between category breadth and accuracy in preschoolers, a relationship that will receive a great deal of attention in the paragraphs to follow. However, returning to the main point of the work of Mervis and co-workers, the difficulty of forming generalizations regarding developmental shifts in breadth and narrowness of categorizations becomes almost insuperable when different dimensions within the same category domain do not obey a common principle. These considerations are also relevant to the matter of individual differences, for different tasks, methods, or dimensions may well generate different correlates. Breadth of categorization may prove to be a less coherent or unified cognitive style than field independence-dependence or reflection-impulsivity.

2.   Developmental Mean Differences
in the Early Preschool Years

Before we turn to the matter of individual differences, however, let us examine what little information is available on age differences in breadth of categorization for children less than 5 years of age. The most relevant and provocative work in this young age group has been carried out by Keith Nelson and his associates. Some of this research has been published (Nelson & Bonvillian, 1973), but a large part of it is still in unpublished form. The Nelson-Bonvillian investigation is based on a sample of 10 middle-class children (5 boys and 5 girls). They ranged in age from 16.2 to 17.5 months at the commencement of a 6 month period of observation.

A total of 16 concept words were selected (for example, barrel, caboose, hedgehog, oiler, snorkel) that were not familiar to the children at the beginning of the study. Furthermore, the parents of the children agreed not to use the words during the course of the investigation. Six objects were selected as exemplars for each of the concept words listed. Three of the six were named by the mother each time the concept was presented; the remaining three were never named. No corrective feedback was permitted. During an experimental session (there were five in all) the experimenter handed the objects directly to the mother at intervals of approximately 45 seconds. The critical dependent variable of interest is the degree to which the child uses the appropriate concept word in the presence of the object exemplars.

Concept learning did occur in these young 18-month-old children, but to a quite limited extent. By the end of the fifth session, the children had correctly labeled almost 20% of the objects. This overall figure, however, conceals a marked difference between objects that had been named by the mother and those that had not, 25 and 12%, respectively. These percentages, in turn, conceal a striking sex difference in favor of the girls. For objects named by the mother, girls named 41% correctly; the corresponding figure for the boys was 10%. For objects not named by the mother, the figures for girls and boys were 17 and 6%, respectively. Nelson and Bonvillian also found an inverse relationship between the naming of an object by the child and the extent to which that object was physically manipulated. As might be expected, boys engaged in more manipulation of the objects than did girls. Finally, mothers' positive reinforcement for naming was significantly associated with name use by the child.[3]

The outcomes of the Nelson and Bonvillian (1973) research strongly support the view that 18-month-old children are exceptionally conservative generalizers. Highly acceptable exemplars of a concept that have not been explicitly named by an adult rarely are named by the child. In sum, it would appear reasonable to characterize the 18-month-old as a narrow categorizer. An unpublished follow-up study by Nelson and his associates of 25 2-year-olds yielded a pattern of findings quite similar to that observed in the 18-month-olds. Although the mean number of objects named was somewhat higher in the 2-year-olds, the trend toward cautious generalization (narrow categorization) was maintained at that age.

A third study carried out by K. E. Nelson and his associates is based on a relatively small sample of five children ranging in age from 2 years and 11 months to 3 years and 11 months.[4] In the training phase, the children were shown six examples for each of seven pictorial concepts, 42 pictures in all. These were all named by the adult examiner and were readily learned by the children in three sessions. The children were then shown "good" concept exemplars that were very similar to or deviated by one, two, or more features from the training stimuli. Also shown were "bad" concept exemplars in which one, two, or three features were clearly wrong relative to the training stimuli. An illustrative set of stimuli is presented in Fig. 4. This portion of the study took place in six sessions over a 2-month period.

The evidence for generalization in the present study is unequivocal. Of 329 "good" exemplars, over 95% were assigned the correct concept label, despite the absence of features in the exemplars that were present in the training stimuli. In short, it is overwhelmingly apparent that the 3-year-olds in the present research were categorizing very broadly. Indeed, even where the exemplars were "poor," concept naming occurred in 82 and 65% of such exemplars with two and three features wrong, respectively, relative to the training stimuli. Hence,

---

[3]This outcome is analogous in some respects to Cicirelli's (1973) evidence that children (kindergarten and second grade) who are aided by older siblings on an object-sorting test tend to exhibit broader categorization than those children who work unaided.

[4]A paper by K. E. Nelson, G. Kovac, and S. Olewitz, "Three-Year-Old's Construction of Broad Concepts on the Basis of Few Concept Exemplars," is currently in preparation.

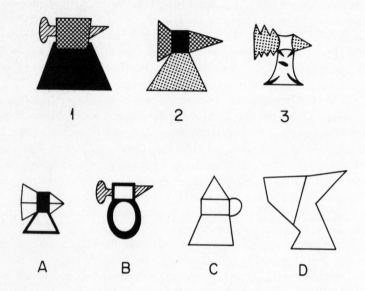

FIG. 4   Examples of stimuli employed in K. E. Nelson's experiment on generalization in 3-year-olds. Items 1, 2, and 3 represent a sample of training stimuli for the concept of "anvils." Item A is a new good example, and B, C, D are bad examples with one, two and three features wrong, respectively.

these children did show some sensitivity to "goodness" as reflected in the declining percentages when moving from "good" to "bad" concept exemplars. Nevertheless, it would be highly appropriate to speak of "overgeneralization" or extremely broad categorizing in the 3-year-old. In marked contrast to the ralatively high percentages reported above, it should be recalled that less than 12% of generalization examples were named by 18-month-olds in the Nelson and Bonvillian (1973) study. There is good reason to believe, then, that broad categorization is characteristic of young children, but not of very young children. Indications are that initial categorizing tendencies (18–24 months) are narrow, hence strongly suggestive that the relationship between age and breadth of categorization may be curvilinear when the developmental continuum is extended from the late infancy period into the early elementary-school years.

Before the evidence for such a developmental curvilinear trend should be accepted, however, a strong cautionary note must be sounded. At the ages (1½ to 2 years) where Nelson observed limited, narrow categorizing, other investigators studying the child's acquisition of semantics in natural settings have reported striking overextensions of word meaning (e.g., Clark, 1973; Donaldson & Wales, 1970). Clark, for example, has offered a "semantic feature" hypothesis whereby the child initially acquires one or two features of a word and thereafter extends it to instances or events in a manner that are considered inappropriate by adult standards. Semantic development, then, consists of the child's progressive acquisition of additional semantic features, the process terminating when the adult category has been achieved. In Clark's (1973) terms, the child's categories "are generally larger since he will use only one or two features critically instead of a whole combination of features [p. 72]." Clark reports a large and diverse variety of children's diary data to support the view that the word meanings of the very young child are characterized by overextension (excessively broad categorizing). The course of semantic development, then, consists of the gradual narrowing down of word meanings as more semantic features are acquired.

There is no question that the foregoing inference is not consistent with the developmental trend observed by Keith Nelson and his associates. It should be stressed, however, that the Clark (1973) position has been convincingly criticized by Katherine Nelson (1973a). She has shown how a single-feature concept can be specific rather than general (as when a dog is defined as "barks" rather than "four legged"). Furthermore, there appear to be examples in Nelson's vocabulary data where a young child has a "narrower rather than a broader category for the adult term—car for toy cars but not real ones, for example, . . ." [p. 100]. Nelson also provides semantic trees for individual children indicative of "quite elaborate semantic systems within a relatively narrow range. . . [p. 101]."

Data obtained from language acquisition research, in sum, does not lend itself to any neat generalization regarding the direction of categorization along a broad-narrow dimension. It is quite clear that all of the child's earliest concepts do not necessarily follow the same sequence. Hence, the consistent trends observed by Keith Nelson and his associates must, in part, reflect the experimental context created to study the phenomenon of interest. As Nelson and Bonvillian (1973) note,

> . . . the child's attention to relevant features underlying a concept might well have been heightened under the structured conditions of the present study as compared with conditions in a child's home, and, as a result, relatively narrow bases for over-generalizations and also relatively few over-generalizations may have occurred in this study [p. 447].

It is rather difficult to understand, however, why "attention to relevant features" should produce narrow categorization when the exemplars of the various concepts are "good" by adult standards. Conceivably, it is the necessity for the child to produce the concept label on demand that causes the difficulty. The competence-performance distinction may well apply in the present circumstances, the child really "knowing" the concept but simply not choosing to emit the label for it at a time convenient to the experimenter. As Nelson (1974b) has observed,

... while it can be stated that naming is dependent upon the existence of concepts, the existence of concepts need not lead directly and easily to naming them [p. 279].

Nelson and Bonvillian acknowledge the presence of marked individual differences in their data but leave the exploration of the bases of such differences for the future. Only the Block and Block (1973) project has examined individual differences in categorization breadth among children of preschool age. That work is based on children no younger than 3 years, an age where the excessively broad categorizing observed by Nelson and his associates has presumably already taken hold. Hence, the study of the bases of individual differences in the categorization breadth of children younger than 3 years remains a task for the future.

3.   Individual Differences

Block and Block have employed four procedures in their assessment of category breadth in 4-year-old children. Two of these are pure "bandwidth" tasks—blues and poggles. In the blues task, the child is shown a standard blue card and is required to categorize as "blue" or "not blue" 27 cards deviating in various degrees from the "blueness" of the standard. The poggles task is formally similar to the blues task, the standard "poggle" consisting of a diamond of a particular angularity and size. Again, 27 variants are provided, the subject having to assign these to the "poggle" or "not-poggle" class. For both of the foregoing tasks, there are nine variants that can be ordered in terms of similarity to the standard and each variant is represented three times in the set of 27. Hence, it is possible to score the child's performance for breadth of categorization (number of variants accepted as blues or poggles) and for consistency of categorization.

A third task employed in the research was a children's version of the McReynolds (1966) Concept Evaluation Test (CET). In this task, the child is shown a series of inkblots and, for each, must indicate which of a diverse set of descriptions appropriately or accurately depict it. A larger number of acceptances or "yes" responses is presumed to reflect "conceptual looseness," but can also be readily interpreted as category breadth. The CET also lends itself to a "conceptual adequacy" score, indicating the degree to which the child's acceptances conform to available norms regarding "good" and "poor" concepts.

Sigel's Object Categorization Test (SOCT) constituted the fourth task within the category breadth domain. It should be noted that this task was administered at ages 3 and 4 years in the Block and Block project, hence permitting an assessment of consistency over a 1-year period. In the SOCT (see Sigel & Olmsted, 1970), an array of 12 common objects is placed before the child (see Fig. 5). One of these is then selected by the examiner as a standard. The child is requested to choose all of the remaining objects that are similar to or belong with the standard in some way and to specify the basis for the selection. This procedure is repeated with seven additional objects from the array used as a standard in turn.[5] Each standard generates an index of breadth—the number of objects grouped with it. The overall category breadth score represents the average of the separate indices. Sigel (in an unpublished manual, 1967) describes a procedure for scoring all of the groupings formed for accuracy or appropriateness.

    a.   Relations between breadth and accuracy.   Consider next the results within the category breadth domain for the 81 boys and 83 girls in the Block and Block sample. Of prime importance is the association between breadth and accuracy or consistency for the four tasks described. The correlations were uniformly negative and, in the large majority of cases, were statistically significant. For the 4-year-old boys, the *r*s were −.66, −.34, −.37, and −.48 (all significant beyond the .05 or .01 levels) for blues, poggles, the CET, and the SOCT, respectively. The corresponding *r*s for the 4-year-old girls were −.76, −.31, −.04, and −.19, respectively. Here the blues and poggles correlations achieved statistical significance (.01 and .05 levels, respectively), but the CET and SOCT correlations fell short. For the 3-year-old boys and girls on the SOCT, the *r*s between breadth and accuracy were −.25 and −.44, respectively, with associated *p* levels of .10 and .01. The overall patterning of these outcomes points to a clear inverse relation between breadth of categorization and the level of consistency or accuracy displayed in deciding whether specific instances belong or do not belong to experimenter-designated or subject-designated categories.

    It is of importance to note that the relationship described above may well achieve its greatest strength in the preschool period, for variance in consistency or accuracy may decline steadily with increasing age.[6] The present outcomes suggest that category boundaries are less firm in early childhood relative to later periods, with the consequence that many preschoolers exhibit inconsistencies for instances located near boundaries or stretch category limits to an inaccuracy-producing extent in order to accommodate particular instances within a category. A reasonable conjecture is that the inverse breadth-consistency (or accuracy) relationship is to some extent a "built-in" phenomenon, for the probability of an inconsistent or inaccurate judgment must necessarily increase as the child moves away from focal exemplars toward the boundaries of a category. There is simply less opportunity for a narrow-categorization child to

---

[5]Note that this procedure corresponds to Sigel's active sort. The general technique also allows for a passive sort in which the investigator creates several successive groupings from the array and requests the child to verbalize the basis for these groupings. The latter procedure appears to be more difficult than the former, and hence the passive sort has typically not been used with preschoolers. An empirical comparison of performance in the active and passive conditions can be found in a study by Singer and Weller (1971) based on a sample of Israeli first graders.

[6]Research by Bieri (1969) with adults indicates that broad categorizers are more accurate in discrimination of line lengths. In a memory for faces task, however, narrow categorizers are more accurate (Messick & Damarin, (1964).

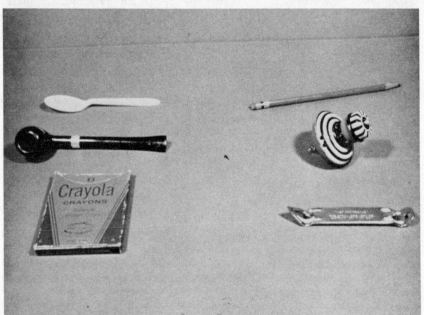

FIG. 5   Common objects employed in the Sigel Object Categorization Task.

display an inconsistent or inaccurate judgment. On the blues task, the correlations were sufficiently high to suggest that a major portion of the variance on the inconsistency index could be attributed to excessive breadth in categorizing. The correlations were considerably lower on the remaining tasks, however, suggesting that error is not an inevitable concomitant of breadth but merely more probable in children with a disposition to form broad categories for diverse arrays of stimulus events.

b. *Generality of breadth and accuracy.* What is the generality of breadth versus narrowness of categorizing in preschool children? The Block and Block evidence indicates that generality is rather weak across the four procedures employed. For boys, the rs ranged from −.03 to .30, with a median r of .19; for girls, the range was −.14 to .47, with a median r of .27. Because only one of the six rs was statistically significant in boys, whereas four of the six were significant in girls, it may be inferred that breadth of categorization is a more coherent dimension in girls than in boys at the age of 4 years.

Generality of consistency or accuracy is even weaker than that observed for category breadth. For the four procedures described, the median r dropped to .17 in boys and .09 in girls. Only one of the six correlations was significant in the case of both boys and girls. Because consistency-accuracy is to a considerable degree a function of the categorizing strategy employed on a particular task, it is hardly surprising that generality of consistency or accuracy has not been found. Given the lack of evidence for a common strategy across tasks, there is little reason to expect the pattern of errors on each task to have much in common.

Despite the low level of intertask generality observed, it is, of course, possible to construct a composite by summating scores across tasks. Block and Block have, in fact, done so for both the breadth and consistency-accuracy dimensions. Not surprisingly, the reliabilities of these composites were not especially high (approximately .50), but it was hoped that the cumulation of variance from breadth and consistency-accuracy across tasks would make possible the discovery of relationships that would otherwise remain concealed. An examination of these relationships is reported in the section to follow.[7]

c. *Stability of assessments.* It will be recalled that one of the procedures— Sigel's Object Categorization Test—was administered to children at the ages of 3 and 4 years. This permits at least a single glimpse of the extent of stability in breadth and accuracy over a 1-year period. In the Block and Block data, the

[7]The consistency-accuracy composite contained one additional measure beyond what. was included in the breadth composite. This was derived from a "tinkertoy" task in which the child was presented with an array of 29 tinkertoys of varying length. The child was required to sort these into three categories—long, short, or middle sized. The consistency score reflects deviations from transitivity in sorting. This task was not included in the breadth composite because of the interdependence of the size of the sorts across the three categories.

coefficients were .14 for breadth and .37 for accuracy. The latter was significant; the former was not. It is therefore evident that 4 year olds did not employ the same strategy on the SOCT that characterized them 1 year previously. Nevertheless, moderate stability in accuracy was observed. The basis for such stability can be traced to the involvement of IQ in the SOCT accuracy score. Correlations between IQ (PPVT and WPPSI) and SOCT accuracy were statistically significant at ages 3 and 4 years for both boys and girls (ranging from .32 to .41). In contrast, correlations between SOCT breadth and IQ were uniformly nonsignificant (rs ranging between $-.05$ and .05). Once again, then, we observe how IQ becomes implicated when a quality criterion is introduced into the domain of cognitive styles.

C.   VALIDATION AT THE PRESCHOOL LEVEL

Do the breadth and the consistency or accuracy of categorizing bear any relation to the child's observable behaviors in the nursery-school classroom? The availability of Q item ratings by teachers in the Block and Block project makes an answer to the question possible. Each of the 100 items in the California Child Q set was examined in relation to the breadth and consistency-accuracy composite scores.

1.   Relation of Breadth to Socioemotional and Task-Oriented Behaviors

Consider first the outcomes for the breadth composite. A quick scan of the correlation coefficients points immediately to a major sex difference in the sheer number of behavioral correlates of categorization breadth. Twenty-two Q items were significantly linked to category breadth in the case of the girls (p at the .05 level or better). For boys, the number of such discriminating items was five (virtually a chance outcome for a 100-item set). Hence, the behavioral implications of category breadth were much more salient in females in the preschool period. The basis for this sex difference is not immediately apparent, but some speculations are offered later (Section IV. D) in the chapter.

Of all the items in the Q set, the one that stands out most clearly as a likely behavioral analog of category breadth is "characteristically tries to stretch limits." This item yielded a significant r of .39 with the breadth composite in the 4-year-old girls. However, this was but one of a variety of socially undesirable characteristics that teachers attributed to girls who are inclined toward broad categorizing. For example, these girls were significantly more likely than their narrow-categorizing peers to be described in the following terms: reacting poorly to stress; having unsatisfactory interpersonal relations with indications of jealousy, taking advantage of others, and a lack of dependability; manifesting aggressiveness, emotional lability, and a rapid personal tempo; displaying an inability to delay gratification, plan ahead, reflect before acting, and adopt a relaxed and easygoing manner. These children were also characterized as being inattentive, unable to concentrate, and lacking in intellectual capacity. The latter relationships are of particular interest in the light of the evidence that IQ measures did not enter into any significant associations with the breadth composite. It appears reasonable that the unsatisfactory interpersonal adjustment and emotional undercontrol of the broad-categorizing girl contributed to an inference of cognitive incapacity on the part of the teacher. In the Block and Block (1973) two-dimensional system—ego resiliency and ego control—the broad-categorizing girls can be clearly designated as low-resilient undercontrollers.

Although the number of significant Q items linked to the breadth composite in boys was at chance level, the items that did discriminate yielded a pattern sufficiently similar to that of the girls to warrant further discussion. Broad-categorizing boys relative to their narrow-categorizing peers were more likely to be described in the following terms: reacting poorly to stress and displaying inappropriate emotional reactions more generally; afraid of being deprived and lacking in self-reliance and confidence; and not ranking high in intellectual capacity. Missing from the boys' characterization but present in the girls' were references to poor interpersonal relations and adjustment, aggressiveness, emotional lability, lack of reflectiveness, and inability to delay gratification. Possible bases for the different patterning of relationships in boys and girls are discussed in Section IV.D, Sex Differences.

In general, it is quite evident that the nursery school teachers who made the Q sorts in the Block and Block research did not find the broad-categorizing child—whether female or male—to be an especially likeable child. There was not a single positive quality attributed to these children. It clearly appears that a style of broad categorization at the preschool level is associated with a pattern of affects and behaviors that nursery-school teachers find disruptive and inappropriate.

2. Relation of Accuracy to Socioemotional and Task-Oriented Behaviors

Consider next the Q item correlates of the consistency-accuracy composite derived from the breadth of categorization tasks. In respect to the number of significant Q items (p less than .05 or better), a sex difference was again apparent. For the girls, 45 items significantly differentiated those who tended toward consistency and accuracy from those who tended toward inconsistency and inaccuracy. The corresponding value for the boys was 14 items. The direction of the sex difference is highly congruent with the previously reported data for the breadth composite. This congruency is no great surprise, for breadth was inversely related to consistency-accuracy. Further testimony to the strength of this inverse relationship concerns the particular Q items that were differentiating. It will be recalled that not a single positive quality was attributed to broad categorizers. In corresponding fashion, not a single unequivocally negative quality was attributed to consistent and accurate children. The list is a veritable parade of virtues in the emotional, interpersonal, and cognitive domains. In short, consistent and accurate children displayed a high level of "ego resiliency" (see Block, 1965). The only indication of a minor flaw in the coping capacity of these children came from the item "when in conflict with others tends to give in," which Block and Block (1973) place in the low-resilient overcontrolled category.

One should not forget, of course, that the consistency-accuracy composite was strongly linked to IQ, and, indeed, it would not be surprising to find the same Q items differentiating high- and low-IQ children. In contrast, breadth, although inversely related to consistency and accuracy, was relatively independent of IQ. Hence, the pattern of low-resilient undercontrol that distinguishes broad categorizers should show little change if an IQ control is employed. It is quite likely, however, that the Q-item correlates of the consistency-accuracy composite would fail to hold up with IQ controlled. In sum, performance on breadth of categorization tasks has both stylistic and ability components. Although a broad categorizer may make more errors, it is nevertheless possible to manifest breadth in categorizing behavior without paying the price of inconsistency and inaccuracy.

D.   SEX DIFFERENCES

An oft-replicated finding in the cognitive-style literature is the greater breadth of categorization manifested by males than females during both childhood and adulthood (Crandall, 1965; Kogan & Wallach, 1964; Pettigrew, 1958; Wallach & Caron, 1959; Wallach & Kogan, 1965). It should be noted that this sex difference has been observed only for tasks of the bandwidth type. Free object-sorting procedures have not yielded a significant sex difference (e.g., Gardner & Moriarty, 1968). The Block and Block data offer the first opportunity to examine mean sex differences in category breadth during the preschool period. These data clearly resemble those reported for older subjects; for all four tasks, 4-year-old males manifested broader categorizing than did 4-year-old females. Only two of these mean sex differences were statistically significant, however. Blues and the SOCT yielded ts significant at the .05 level; the CET and poggles tasks did not yield a significant mean difference, nor did the SOCT produce a significant sex difference at age 3 years. On the whole, it seems fair to assert that the oft-reported sex difference in breadth of categorization in later childhood and adulthood can be discerned in children as young as 4 years.

For very young children—Nelson and Bonvillian's (1973) 18-month-olds—the sex difference is reversed. It will be recalled that girls were much more likely than boys to generalize concept words to previously unnamed exemplars. In the context of the Nelson-Bonvillian work, categorization breadth reflects superior performance, in contrast to the inverse relationship between breadth and accuracy observed later in the preschool period. From the foregoing perspective, 18-month-old girls can be considered developmentally advanced relative to their male age peers. Once again, then, the evidence points to female superiority at the preschool level.[8]

In addition to the mean sex difference, some effort must be made to explain the sex difference in the pattern of correlations described in the preceding sections. It will be recalled that breadth of categorization proved to be more strongly linked to the domain of personality and social behavior for girls than for boys. A number of possible explanations for the observed difference can be advanced, although none can qualify as definitive.

The most basic of these possible explanations is psychometric. Recall that the relationships among the four measures of breadth showed greater coherence in girls than boys. The correlations between each of these measures and the composite index ranged from .53 to .71 in the sample of boys and from .65 to .79 in the sample of girls. Hence, the composite index possessed a larger proportion of genuine breadth variance in the case of girls than in the case of boys, thereby attenuating relationships for the latter between the composite and the CCQ items. As to the issue of why there is more coherence in the category breadth domain for girls than for boys, one may speculate that this is a further example of the more rapid developmental advance of girls previously demonstrated for the field dependence-independence and reflection-impulsivity dimensions. More specifically, it can be argued that a general stylistic dimension of category breadth versus narrowness emerges somewhat earlier for girls than boys. The indication that all four breadth indices are significantly associated with consistency or accuracy in boys, whereas only two of the four are so associated in girls tends to support that point of view. One may clearly expect breadth and consistency or accuracy to become progressively disassociated from each other with development, and, in that respect, 4-year-old girls are somewhat more advanced developmentally than 4-year-old boys.

The argument developed so far, although helping to explicate the differential magnitude of cognition-personality relationships across the sexes, nevertheless does not explain why these relationships assume the particular character observed earlier. The 4-year-old males in the Block and Block research manifested broader categorizing than did the 4-year-old females. As we have seen, broad

[8]Strong consideration must also be given to the possibility that the observed sex differences in the Nelson-Bonvillian study have little relevance to category breadth as such. Instead, the results may reflect the more rapid maturing of vocal-verbal behavior in females that has been observed in other contexts (see Kagan, 1971; McCall et al., 1972).

categorizing was linked to low ego resilience and ego undercontrol. Some years ago, Maccoby (1966) offered a hypothetical model suggesting that girls who are more impulsive (that is, less controlled and hence more similar to boys) exhibit higher levels of intellectual functioning than their more controlled female peers. The Block and Block data not only failed to support such a model, they actually were in a direction opposite to the prediction derived from the model. Girls who were broad categorizers (hence more like boys) were not superior to their narrow-categorizing same-sexed peers on any of the intellective indices represented in the Block and Block project. In fact, the teachers of the broad-categorizing girls judged them to be less intellectually competent than the girls who manifested a more narrow style of categorizing, despite the absence of actual IQ differences between the two subgroups.

It it evident, then, that undercontrol or impulsiveness does not have to impart a cognitive advantage to the preschool girl. The behavioral correlates of broad categorizing in preschool girls were not highly prized by teachers, who quite clearly found these children disruptive and troublesome. It is not inconceivable that these children violated teachers' expectancies regarding "appropriate" behavior for 4-year-old girls. One should also allow for the possibility that greater undercontrol was expected and sanctioned in boys by virtue of sex-typed norms. This might contribute to the lesser overlap between socioemotional and cognitive attributes in the Q-sort data observed in the boys relative to the girls.

There is a reasonable likelihood that the relationships described above dissipate as development proceeds. On the assumption that breadth of categorization gradually becomes less tied to consistency or accuracy, the weakening of the link between broad categorizing and low ego resiliency should necessarily follow. Followup data from the Block and Block project will permit an eventual test of this hypothesis.

E.   CONCLUSIONS AND IMPLICATIONS

Unlike the case of the two cognitive styles considered previously—field independence-dependence and reflection-impulsivity—where downward extensions in age to the preschool level were, to a considerable extent, feasible, the breadth of categorization domain in preschoolers offers few obvious parallels to that style in its functioning at older age levels. With regard to developmental changes in breadth, most of the published evidence has favored the view that, prior to adulthood, individuals become broader as they get older. Yet the Block and Block data clearly indicate that category breadth at the 4-year-old level is associated with a pattern of maladaptive coping in the nursery-school setting. In contrast, the research of Keith Nelson and his associates with children 3 years of age and younger strongly suggests that breadth of categorization is adaptive for concept learning. Such findings strongly suggest that the breadth of early childhood is far from identical to the breadth of later childhood and adulthood. Longitudinal data are essential to a determination of the change and stability of breadth measures from early to later childhood. It will be recalled that the stability coefficient for the SOCT between the ages of 3 and 4 years was exceedingly low (r = .14). For a partial sample of 41 children, however, Block and Block (1973) report a stability coefficient of .50 between the ages of 4 and 5 years on the McReynolds CET. This reflects a considerably higher level of stability, but one simply does not know, of course, whether such early stability is peculiar to the CET or generalizes more broadly.

Despite the modest intertask correlations observed in the Block and Block research, the use of a composite nevertheless generates a host of Q-item correlates. These outcomes represent a genuine contribution, for there has been a dearth of knowledge regarding the cognitive and socioemotional correlates of category breadth in preschool children. Indeed, there have been few comparable studies at any age level.

In research conducted with young adults a number of years ago, Kogan and Wallach (1964) included the Pettigrew (1958) category-width questionnaire in their battery of risk-taking, cognitive-judgmental, personality, and ability measures. A rather striking parallel to the Block and Block work concerns the emergence of significant relationships in the female, but not the male, sample. Further parallels are difficult to draw, however, given the strikingly different correlates examined. The general outcome of the Kogan-Wallach research indicated that the women who categorized broadly were lower in judgmental confidence and more conservative on most of the decision-making indices. Whereas the Block and Block 4-year-old broad-categorizing females could be classified as low ego-resilient undercontrollers, the adult females with comparable categorizing tendencies in the Kogan and Wallach research appear overcontrolled by the Block and Block criteria.

A major difficulty in the category-breadth domain is explaining the psychological meaning of a broad or narrow choice. In the case of the Pettigrew task, Kogan and Wallach (1964) argued that breadth reflects caution because there is at least one highly deviant instance for most events, and hence, to omit such instances from the category represents a highly risky course of action. Elsewhere, Wallach and Kogan (1965), employing a children's version of the Pettigrew questionnaire, maintained that breadth reflects a tolerance for deviant instances. Such an interpretation was consistent with the observation that breadth related significantly to divergent thinking in children approximately 10 to 11 years of age. Still another interpretation is obviously required to account for the Block and Block and Nelson-Bonvillian outcomes. At the later preschool level, breadth of categorization in part reflects a lack of clarity regarding the outer limits of a category. The consequence is inconsistency or inaccuracy in the assignment of instances to that category. Early in the preschool years, however, categorization breadth seems to represent an ability to generalize concept labels to previously unnamed but appropriate exemplars.

Although the various interpretations advanced above are not entirely compatible with one another, their link to different stages of the life span implies that category breadth may not have the same psychological significance in early childhood, later childhood, and young adulthood. With increasing age, a disposition toward broad categorizing is more likely to reflect a stylistic preference or conscious strategy rather than an incapacity to categorize narrowly. It is dubious whether the preschool child recognizes the subjectivity of the options available in the categorizing task; he or she is more likely to be locked into a broad or narrow style as a reflection of more pervasive motivational dispositions. With growth (and resultant differentiation), the categorizing task is likely to involve strategic choices, and their connection with the deeper levels of the personality is markedly attenuated. Even if personality or motivational linkages continue to be manifest, the particular dimensions implicated will probably change in the light of the differing psychological meaning of broad versus narrow categorizing in younger and older individuals.

In referring to a general disposition toward broad or narrow categorizing, it is important not to lose sight of the differences as well as the similarities between the tasks employed. The distinction between object-sorting and bandwidth procedures has already been discussed. Even within the bandwidth domain, however, the content and/or structure of the task may have the effect of introducing extraneous sources of variation that work against intertask generality. The Pettigrew task, for example, requires quantitative judgment, and it has been observed that the broad categorizer performs better on certain kinds of quantitative aptitude tests (Messick & Kogan, 1965). The blues and poggles tasks involve subtle perceptual discriminations, and it is possible that the higher inconsistency of the broad categorizer on these procedures partially reflects reduced capacity to discriminate and hence to recall how instances have been classified previously. The McReynolds Concept Evaluation Test depends on yes versus no responses from the subject, with the former always reflective of broad categorizing. Hence, there is likely to be some acquiescence variance linked to breadth on the CET. Kogan (1971) discusses evidence from a number of studies showing how the presence of such extraneous variance can sometimes produce inverse associations between breadth and IQ.

Task differences, of course, are just as important in delineating the nature of developmental change as in accounting for the patterning of individual differences. We have seen how inferences regarding the direction of such developmental change in the use of natural language concepts can assume strikingly different forms as a function of the task format. With pictorial stimulus material, categorization proceeds from greater narrowness to greater breadth (although even this trend can be influenced by the particular concepts and instances employed). When natural language concepts are examined via a semantic memory procedure, the developmental trend seems to assume the opposite direction—breadth to narrowness.

The foregoing differences between tasks cannot be ignored in any future attempt to locate possible infant precursors of a broad versus narrow-categorizing style. Semantic recall, perceptual discrimination, quantitative estimation, and acquiescence are not likely to follow an identical developmental course. Whatever expectations one may have held to the effect that a style becomes more unified and coherent as chronological age decreases receives little support from the research surveyed in the present section. The generality of breadth of categorization is no stronger in 4-year-olds than in young adults. At the same time, it has been shown that there is enough shared variance at the preschool level to generate highly meaningful composites of breadth and consistency-accuracy. The socioemotional correlates of breadth of categorization uncovered in the Block and Block research represent an important breakthrough in elucidating the psychological significance of a cognitive style. These findings, along with the research on younger children by Nelson and his associates, constitute a solid anchoring point for those who should wish to explore the roots of broad and narrow categorizing in infancy and very early childhood.

V

Styles of Conceptualization

A. GENERAL BACKGROUND

When an individual is given an array of objects to be grouped, the investigator is not limited to the study of the number and size of the groupings formed. Instead, the individual under test can be asked to specify the rationale for the various groupings produced. It is these rationales that constitute styles of conceptualization. This is not to imply that such styles can only be examined within the context of tasks that simultaneously allow for an assessment of breadth. Procedures have in fact been developed for measuring conceptual style directly. The most popular of these has been the Conceptual Styles Test (CST) of Kagan *et al.* (1963). Each item in the test consists of a triad of pictures, where possible pairings are analytic-descriptive (common elements), inferential-categorical (common class membership), and relational (thematic linkage). It is essential to note that the foregoing threefold distinction does not begin to exhaust the variety of classification schemes imposed on subjects' verbal reports of reasons for grouping diverse arrays of stimuli. As Kogan (1971) has indicated, some investigators have preferred to concentrate on the accuracy or logical adequacy of sorting whereas others have been attracted to the abstract-concrete distinction.

For a variety of reasons, this chapter emphasizes the scheme initially proposed by Kagan *et al.* (1963). First, the threefold distinction—analytic, categorical, relational—is clearly stylistic in nature in the sense that the **three** modes seem to reflect individual preferences rather than capacities. Second, the scheme can be flexibly employed with free and constrained sorting tasks as well as with the triads of the Conceptual Styles Test. Third, the scoring is quite straightforward and reliable and does not entail the kinds of evaluative inferences underlying the abstractness-concreteness dimension. Finally, the Kagan *et al.* (1963) schema has been employed in both developmental and individual-difference contexts and hence is quite consistent with the dual focus of this volume.

In their earlier treatment of styles of conceptualization, Kagan and Kogan (1970) and Kogan (1971) adopted a relativistic stance in regard to conceptual styles. Those authors insisted that the meaning of an analytic, categorical, or relational response depends largely on the nature of the stimulus array and the mode of sorting (for example, pictorial versus verbal stimuli, pairing within triads versus free sorting of a large array). This implied that any statement regarding a child's standing on an analytic dimension, for example, could not be generalized beyond the particular assessment procedure employed. It now appears that some generalizability exists, after all, for Denney (1971) observed significant consistency of stylistic preferences in elementary-school children across a modified Conceptual Styles Test (triads) and the Olver-Hornsby picture-sorting task (free grouping) described by Bruner *et al.* (1966).

Despite the indication in Kagan *et al.* (1963) that the CST is tapping stylistic preferences rather than differences in capacity (children seem capable of forming alternative pairings within each triad), a value bias in favor of the analytically inclined child has been evident until quite recently. Baird and Bee (1969), using candy reinforcement with first- and second-grade children, found that they could train analytic and nonanalytic children to move in nonanalytic and analytic directions, respectively. Those authors noted, however, that the analytic children on a posttest showed a partial reinstatement of their analytic disposition, whereas the nonanalytic children adhered to their newly acquired analytic style. The outcome, in brief, suggested that stable shifts are more likely to occur in developmentally "mature" as opposed to "immature" directions. This clearly represents the terminology of a Type II cognitive style.

More recent research has seriously undermined the foregoing value bias. D. R. Denney (1972) has pointed to a critical methodological flaw in the Baird and Bee investigation: the reinforcement procedures were more specific in the case of analytic training, which could readily account for the differential stability of shifts favoring the more "sophisticated" style. In his own study, based on second-grade boys exposed to an adult modeling analytic and relational responses, Denney observed that the latter modeling condition had a stronger immediate effect on analytic boys than did the former modeling condition on relational boys. In a follow-up approximately 2 weeks later the relational boys retained their newly acquired analytic style at full strength, whereas the analytic boys manifested a slight movement away from their newly acquired relational style. Although this latter shift was quite small in absolute terms, it is of interest that Denney nevertheless characterized the analytic and relational modes as more and less "sophisticated," respectively (1972, p. 117). It represents a further tribute to the strong positive value connotations evoked by the analytic label.

Possibly the most damaging evidence against the value bias typical of the present cognitive-style domain is contained in a paper by Davis (1971). That author employed the Sigel (1967) Conceptual Styles Test (SCST), a more sophisticated version of the CST, with samples of students drawn from the fifth, eighth, and eleventh grades and college. Davis requested subjects to note all possible pairings in the triad, not simply the most preferred pairing. In scoring the SCST, it should be noted that an additional conceptualizing mode has been added—"descriptive global." This refers to pairings based on objective characteristics of the stimuli as a whole (for example, shape, size). The grouping designated "analytic" in the original CST is relabeled as "descriptive part-whole" in the SCST.[1]

The developmental trends reported by Davis (1971) give no indication of a decline in relational groupings over the age span examined. Indeed, such groupings exceeded the percentage of analytic responses at all four age levels. Categorical and descriptive-global groupings were most and least frequent, respectively, in each age group. Furthermore, there was no indication of highly dominant stylistic preferences in the data of individual subjects. Instead, the data quite clearly showed that particular triads of the test "pulled" particular kinds of groupings, hence producing considerable intraindividual variation in choice of conceptualizing modes. Indeed, this intraindividual variation increased with the age of the respondent. In sum, it is strikingly clear from the Davis data that individuals do not necessarily abandon a more "primitive" conceptual style in favor of a more "sophisticated" one as development proceeds. Instead, alternative conceptualizing modes remain in the repertoire and are invoked in accordance with stimulus requirements.

Further evidence against the claim that the analytic-descriptive mode reflects a sophisticated cognitive approach is contained in a study by White (1971). That author employed an object-sorting task in which children of kindergarten age and second, fourth, sixth, and eighth graders had to form 10 successive groupings (reusing the same objects if necessary). The bases for grouping were scored as descriptive, inferential, or relational. The first of these (initially called "analytic") manifested a gradual progressive decline in incidence from kindergarten through eighth grade. In contrast, inferential grouping increased and relational grouping decreased from younger to older ages, but virtually all of the change occurred between kindergarten and second grade. Mean differences from the latter through eighth grade were negligible. Despite the different tasks employed in the Davis (1971) and White (1971) studies—triads and object sorting, respectively—the outcomes of the two investigations are rather consistent in demonstrating that specific conceptualizing modes do not disappear over the course of development, although their incidence varies as a function of age and the nature of the conceptual task.

[1] According to Sigel, Jarman, and Hanesian (1967), the term "analytic" has been dropped in order to emphasize the nature of the stimuli rather than the presumed cognitive process. Note further that the "relational" category has been expanded to "relational-contextual."

Research on school-age children points unequivocally to the preferential character of conceptual styles. We are now prepared to ask whether the conceptual styles of preschool children retain the preferential form. It is, of course, possible that very young children do not as yet have alternative conceptualizing modes open to them. Indeed, a number of investigators (e.g., Bruner *et al.*, 1966; Inhelder & Piaget, 1964; Vygotsky, 1962) have proposed that developmental stages characterize conceptual function in early childhood. From such a perspective, the kinds of groupings formed by preschoolers indicate what they are capable of doing, not what they prefer to do. In the subsequent section, the preferential style versus capacity distinction at the preschool level is examined. The issue of meaningful individual differences in the conceptualizing of very young children—whether stylistic preferences or capacities—also receives due consideration.

B.   ASSESSMENT AT THE PRESCHOOL LEVEL

1.   Modifications of the Conceptual Styles Test for Preschoolers

In their study of styles of conceptualization in preschoolers, Sigel *et al.* (1967) observed that the original CST (Kagan *et al.*, 1963) was too difficult for a sample of middle-class 4-year-old children. Accordingly, Sigel and his associates modified the CST by adding a fourth picture that could serve as a standard, the child being assigned the task of selecting one of three other pictures that "goes with, or is like" the standard in some way. Only one such choice was permitted per item and, for each choice, the child had to specify the reason for his or her choice. Scoring of these reasons followed the expanded scheme described earlier—descriptive part-whole, descriptive-global, relational-contextual, and categorical-inferential. An illustrative item is shown in Fig. 6.

The mean incidence from highest to lowest of the four conceptual modes in 4- and 5-year-old boys and girls without exception were as follows: descriptive part-whole, relational-contextual, categorical-inferential, and descriptive-global. The ordering obtained as well as the lack of any significant change from 4 to 5 years of age in the incidence of descriptive part-whole or relational-contextual preference again calls into question the oft-presumed "sophistication" of analytic and "primitiveness" of nonanalytic modes of grouping.

Little additional research has been carried out with the revised version of the CST described above. Instead, Sigel and his associates turned their attention to another procedure—the SOCT described in Chapter IV (see Fig. 5). The rationale for the switch to the SOCT has been described by Sigel (1972). In brief, Sigel and his co-workers (e.g., Sigel, Anderson, & Shapiro, 1966; Sigel & McBane, 1967) observed that preschool lower-class black children experienced considerable difficulty in grouping pictorial representations of persons, animals,

FIG. 6   Sample item from Sigel's modification of the Conceptual Styles Test.

88

plants, and objects. Use of three-dimensional objects with these children, in contrast, produced grouping behavior virtually indistinguishable from that of black middle-class children of the same age. This research demonstrated that certain subgroups of young children do not yet possess the competence required to manipulate representations of objects on conceptualization tasks. These outcomes necessarily implied that an object-sorting task appropriate for all children demanded the use of actual three-dimensional objects.

A review of research based on Sigel's Object Categorization Test has been prepared by Lindstrom and Shipman (1972). That report also discusses the SOCT results in the ETS longitudinal study. In respect to scoring of the SOCT, it should be observed that Sigel has returned to a threefold schema by eliminating the distinction between descriptive part-whole and descriptive-global groupings. That category is now simply labelled as "descriptive." This essentially represents a return to the scoring scheme of the original CST. Before this classification can be applied, of course, it is essential that the child produce a modicum of scorable grouping responses. Preschool children often fail in that respect, and hence the number of groupings formed becomes an important variable in its own right.

It goes without saying that the child must have achieved a minimal level of classification skill as a prerequisite for the assessment of classification style. A particularly surprising outcome of the ETS longitudinal study was the indication that children ranging in age from approximately 3 to 6 years, although capable of labeling objects correctly and grouping them, could not provide reasons for their groupings. Lindstrom and Shipman further indicated that the rationales occasionally provided by the children did not seem to match discernible characteristics of the objects included in the grouping. Accordingly, no effort was made to apply the scoring categories for conceptual styles to the data in hand. Instead, analysis was confined to grouping ability as such, and it was not too surprising to observe that this ability was loaded on a "g" factor in Shipman's (1972) factor analysis.[2]

In striking contrast to the foregoing outcomes, the Block and Block (1973) data did lend themselves to scoring for conceptual style. This may reflect the higher SES levels of children in the latter project and/or variation in the context of task administration such that scorable data (for conceptual style) were generated in one project but not the other. The performance of the children in the ETS longitudinal study is particularly surprising in light of the fact that Sigel developed the three-dimensional form of the SOCT to facilitate grouping

[2]In a sample of Israeli first graders, Singer and Weller (1971) observed that grouping ability was associated with middle (as opposed to lower) social status and Western (as opposed to Middle Eastern) ethnic origin. Of further interest is the evidence that girls significantly exceed boys on the foregoing grouping variable, suggesting that the striking evidence (reviewed earlier) for the more rapid cognitive development of girls at the preschool level may be extrapolated to include 6-year-old first graders for certain selected variables.

in lower class black children of preschool age. Evidently, the use of three-dimensional materials enhances grouping in underprivileged children but, as Sigel (1972) himself has observed, there is no guarantee that the child is able to provide an adequate verbal rationale for his grouping.[3]

The deficits exhibited by preschool disadvantaged children are not necessarily immutable, for Sigel (1972) has demonstrated that classification training (20 min. a day for 20 school days) focused on attributes of objects and similarities between objects can raise the level of and the variety of bases for grouping as well as the likelihood of appropriate verbal rationales for groupings formed. However, such changes appear to be confined to three-dimensional materials, as little generalization to pictorial representations was found. Furthermore, a follow-up 8 months later indicated little change in the trained group but enough improvement in the control group to wipe out prior differences. The vitiation of the training effect points to the weak "staying power" of short-term interventions that receive no additional reinforcements in the child's customary educational environment.

2.   Developmental Mean Differences

Let us now return to the properties of the scores generated by the SOCT. In the case of the number of grouping responses—the relevant score in the ETS longitudinal study (Lindstrom & Shipman, 1972)—the older children (in a median split) exceeded the younger children. Reliabilities (coefficient alpha) for total grouping exceeded .90 in both the first- and second-year administration. The consistency of the total grouping score across the 1-year period was quite low, however ($r = .23$). Lindstrom and Shipman also report modest generality for total groupings on the SOCT and toy- and block-sorting tasks (rs in the 30s).

Consider next the properties of the SOCT style scores obtained in the Block and Block project. For boys and girls at 3 and 4 years of age, the preponderant proportion of scorable responses (approximately two-thirds and three-quarters for the 3- and 4-year-olds, respectively) were classified as descriptive. The remainder of the responses were relational or categorical, the former exceeding

[3]The inability of the child to provide such verbal rationales has been insightfully explained by Blank (1975). That author has shown that "why" questions hold a different meaning for preschoolers relative to the intended meaning for adults. When the preschooler is asked the reason for putting various objects together to form a group, he or she may well interpret the question as a request for one's internal motivation rather than as a request to focus on specific attributes of the stimulus situation. Hence a typical response from the preschooler may be "because I like them together that way" or "because I'm smart." In the light of Blank's observations, it is less surprising that Shipman (1972) and Sigel (1972) have not obtained scorable verbal rationales than that the Blocks have been able to do so for children as young as 3 years.

the latter in three of the four groups. Their incidence was about equal in the 4-year-old girls.

Once more, we observe that descriptive groupings are quite common at an early age. One must keep in mind that descriptive responses include both the part-whole and global varieties, and it is the latter that are more prevalent in early childhood. In their discussion of the ETS longitudinal study, Lindstrom and Shipman (1972) note that the few verbalized rationales for grouping provided by their preschool sample concerned color and form. These are global, immediately perceptible properties that may have little relation to the similarity of structural elements presumably tapped by a genuinely analytical approach to the object-sorting task. The relative rarity of the categorical response in the Blocks' data in conjunction with its relative popularity in older subjects suggests rather strongly that cognitive "sophistication" may lie in that direction. A number of investigators, in fact, treat the categorical superordinate form of grouping as a sign of developmental maturity in the conceptualizing domain (e.g., Bruner *et al.*, 1966; Inhelder & Piaget, 1964; Vygotsky, 1962).

3. Stability of Assessments

What is the stability of conceptual style at the preschool level? Because the SOCT was administered at 3 and 4 years of age in the Blocks' project, stability coefficients could be computed. For 38 girls, these were .34, .09, and .41 for the descriptive, relational, and categorical modes, respectively. The first and last of these achieved statistical significance at the .05 level. For the 27 boys, however, stability was negligible—rs of $-.06$, $-.03$, and $-.01$ for the three modes in the sequence listed above. In sum, there is modest stability in the case of the girls but none whatever for boys between the ages of 3 and 4 years. Such evidence is consistent with the view that girls exhibit greater developmental maturity than boys at the ages indicated in the sense that a reasonably stable style has emerged for girls although not for boys. It will be recalled that comparable findings were obtained in the other cognitive-style domains.

4. Stages of Classification

Thus far, our attention has been confined to children no younger than 3 years of age. Although children younger than 3 years may not be able to verbalize their reasons for grouping stimuli in particular ways, it nevertheless would be of considerable interest to observe whether such children manifest a systematic grouping tendency of any kind.

Both Vygotsky (1962) and Inhelder and Piaget (1964), employing primarily geometric stimuli varying in shape, color, and size, have offered detailed descriptions of fine-grained shifts in grouping behavior over the developmental span of childhood (beginning at approximately 2-3 years of age). Both propose a sequence of "stages" through which the child passes on the way to "true classification." For Vygotsky, the first stage is characterized by "syncretic heaps" in which the child groups blocks randomly or on the basis of spatial contiguity. The next major stage prior to mature classification is the "complex." This in turn is divided into a sequence of substages or phases that represent the child's movement from rudimentary efforts to group by similarity to the point where the child can group on the basis of a single consistent attribute.

Vygotsky's procedure consisted of giving a particular block a nonsense syllable name and then asking the child to select other blocks with the same name. Inhelder and Piaget, in contrast, simply requested their subjects to group the blocks that were alike or belonged together. Those authors also describe three main developmental stages, the first two characterized by substages and the third reflective of mature classification. The first is labeled "graphic collections" and is characterized by groupings that take the form of spatial arrangements or designs in which criteria of similarity between blocks is secondary. "Nongraphic collections" constitute the second stage. The child now groups entirely on the basis of similarity but, in the earlier phases of this stage, does not use similarity criteria consistently or group all relevant objects exhaustively. Eventually, the child reaches the final stage of consistent grouping on a particular criterion with subsequent subdivison on a second criterion.

5.   Critical Tests of Stage Theories

Explicit in the work of Inhelder and Piaget and implicit in Vygotsky's is the view that young preschool children (age 4 years and below) have not yet achieved the final stage of "true classification." N. W. Denney (1972a, b), in research based on 2-, 3-, and 4-year-old children, has clearly demonstrated that the capacities of these preschoolers has been understimated by the "stage" theorists. In Denney's (1972a) first study, both Vygotsky's verbal-labeling procedure and Inhelder and Piaget's free-grouping procedure were employed with children of 2 and 4 years of age (as well as with older children and adolescents). In the verbal-labeling procedures, all 4-year-olds grouped the geometric stimuli on the basis of form, behavior consistent with that of the 6-, 8-, 12-, and 16-year-olds. In the case of the 2-year-olds, approximately 50% also grouped by form, the remaining 50% failing to use a similarity criterion.

Additional categories were needed to accommodate the diversity of response generated by the free-grouping procedure. Children grouped the blocks by form or color, or they used blocks of the same color or of the same form to build some construction. This last category, "building with similarity" was fairly common in the 2- and 4-year-olds. By 4 years of age, however, all children were using similarity criteria for grouping, whereas approximately 45% of the 2-year-olds failed to do so. Of the remaining 55% one-fourth grouped by form or color and about 30% resorted to building with similarity. Of further interest in

Denney's data was the decreasing heterogeneity over age; more than three-fourths of the responses by age 12 years represented grouping by form.

Denney (1972a) argues persuasively that her data do not support the stage conceptions of Vygotsky or Inhelder and Piaget. Recognizing, however, that her use of fairly broad age categories (no subjects between the ages of 2 and 4 years) may have obscured the emergency of stages, Denney (1972b) reports a second study using the free-grouping procedure of Inhelder and Piaget with samples of 2-, 3-, and 4-year olds.[4] The use of this constrained age range also allowed for more refined distinctions among scoring categories than was possible when the age spread extended from 2 to 16 years. Using Inhelder and Piaget's categories (pregraphic responses, graphic collections, nongraphic collections, and true classification), systematic trends could be discerned across the age span examined. Particularly salient is the sharp decline in pregraphic (failure to group) responses from 2 to 3 years of age (a decline from approximately 40 to 5%). Consistent with the foregoing is the increase in "true classification" from about 3% of the responses at age 2 years to 15% at age 3 years and 30% at age 4 years. Although such findings conform to Inhelder and Piaget's expectations, Denney observes that graphic and nongraphic collections did not display any systematic relation to age, hence casting serious doubt on the former's stage-sequence view of classification behavior. In all fairness to Inhelder and Piaget, however, it should be noted that cross-sectional age trends cannot invalidate a "stage" position. Longitudinal data would be necessary in such a case. Nevertheless, the evidence that both graphic and nongraphic collections increase between the ages of 2 and 3 years is damaging to the view that the former precedes the latter in the development of classification skills.

On the presumption that "graphic collections" do not constitute a separate stage in the development of free classification, Denney (1972b) offers a new scheme for categorizing the data on grouping across the age range of 2-4 years. She distinguishes three stages: (1) no similarity, (2) incomplete similarity (where only a fraction of the objects are grouped according to similarity criteria), and (3) complete similarity (the entire stimulus array is grouped on the basis of consistent similarity criteria). When the data were grouped in the foregoing manner, a highly significant relationship between age and category stage emerged. Across the three stages of "no similarity," "incomplete similarity," and "complete similarity," the percentages of response were as follows: for 2-year-olds, 50, 45, and 5% respectively; for 3-year-olds, 11, 53, and 36% respectively; for 4-year-olds, 11, 25, and 64% respectively. Each age group contained 36 children about equally divided by sex.

Also discrepant from Inhelder and Piaget is the evidence reported by Denney (1972b) indicating that the child's use of one or two dimensions (selected from color, form, and size) is independent of age. According to Inhelder and Piaget,

---

[4]No indication is given as to why the Vygotsky verbal-labeling procedure was dropped in the second study, hence precluding the opportunity to examine the possible emergence of stages from that perspective.

grouping on one dimension should precede a further subdivision into two dimensions for grouping purposes. Again, longitudinal data are required to definitively settle the issue, but Denney's cross-sectional data clearly do not favor the Inhelder-Piaget position.

In sum, Denney has demonstrated that children as young as 2 years of age (about one-half of a middle-class sample) are capable of abstracting such attributes as color, form, or size from an array of geometric stimuli and using them to group by similarity. However, with few exceptions, such grouping was not optimally efficient as the children did not sort the entire array in a consistent fashion. By 3 years of age, the large majority of the children employed similarity criteria for sorting, a sizeable number doing so with optimal efficiency. Finally, by 4 years of age, exhaustive, efficient grouping by similarity had become the modal response.

An obvious question posed by Denney's research is the basis for failure to group by complete similarity at 2 and 3 years of age. Again, it is important to ask whether the child's performance is reflective of a basic incapacity or a stylistic preference for an alternative mode of response. If the latter should prove to be the case, appropriate short-term training might readily produce grouping by complete similarity in 2- and 3-year-olds. Denney and Acito (1974) have carried out such a study of classification training in which the experimenter served as a model. On two successive occasions, the experimenter exhaustively grouped the stimuli by shape and size in the presence of children who had failed to group by complete similarity on a pretest. A control group was permitted to play with the forms prior to the posttest.[5] The first posttest made use of the same forms employed for the pretest and training. A second posttest, following immediately, used a different set of geometric forms, thus permitting a test of generalization or transfer effects.

Results obtained by Denney and Acito (1974) strongly support the view that children as young as 2 years of age possess the capacity to group geometric forms by similarity. Of the 17 children exposed to the model, 13 subsequently met the criterion of complete similarity grouping on the immediate posttest. Only three of the 17 control children satisfied the above criterion. On the second posttest (the generalization task), 11 of the 13 children cited above maintained their level of grouping by complete similarity. The corresponding proportion for the control children was two out of three. It is therefore evident that the performance of the children in the modeling condition cannot be attributed to sheer imitation; of the 13 children who were successful in grouping the training materials by complete similarity, 11 (85%) transferred this grouping behavior to a completely new set of materials (which included a new dimension—pattern replacing shape).

[5] A condition of reinforcement for similarity matching was also included in the study but it proved relatively ineffective and hence is not discussed here.

It is therefore strikingly evident that children are attuned to the physical dimensions of geometric forms and able to use them to form exhaustive and accurate groupings at an age considerably younger than anticipated from the work of Inhelder and Piaget (1964). Denney (1972b) attributes the precocity of her samples to the rapid growth of early childhood education on the American scene, much of which is concerned with teaching children about similarities and differences among objects. The "Sesame Street" television program (Ball & Bogatz, 1972) is a prime example of such an effort. Of course, this would not explain why some 2- and 3-year-olds spontaneously grouped by similarity, whereas others had to be trained to do so. Denney and her colleagues have not explored the issue of differential exposure to educational influences in the samples studied. Hence, the basis for individual differences in the grouping behavior of children as young as 2 or 3 years remains an unknown in the research described. Nevertheless, it is of considerable importance to discover that 2-year-olds who spontaneously deal with geometric forms in a complementary manner (for example, making designs or constructions) can with a minimum of training flexibly alter their grouping behavior to sort the forms by similarity of color, shape, size, or pattern.

6.   Classification in Infants One to Two Years of Age

Given the evidence that about 50% of middle-class children in the age range of 2-3 years spontaneously group by complete similarity (with most of the remaining 50% easily trained to do so), it naturally follows that one should like to know about the grouping capacities of children 24 months of age and younger. The youngest subject in the Denney research was approximately 26 months of age. Such research, at first blush, would appear to pose difficult, if not insuperable, methodological problems given the limited verbal comprehension of such young children and infants. When working with subjects less than 2 years of age, one can no longer count on the child's grasp of explicit instructions, and so it is of considerable interest to observe how investigators have coped with this problem. Two relevant studies have been published (Ricciuti, 1965; Nelson, 1973b).

Ricciuti's research was carried out with three samples of infants, 16 each at 12, 18, and 24 months of age. Schematic drawings of the stimulus materials and the standard arrangement for their presentation are shown in Fig. 7. In Task I, the contrast was comprised of four yellow cubical "stringing" beads and four dark, gray, slightly malleable clay balls. In Task II, the stimuli were red masonite cutouts, four large and four small, all similarly shaped. In Task III, four large and four small masonite cutouts were again used, but shapes and colors within each set varied. These nonrelevant cues were intended to make this task more difficult than the preceding one. Finally, Task IV cutouts consisted of four identical ellipses and four identical parallelograms. All eight were yellow and of approximately equal area.

For each task, the objects were placed on a tray before the infant in the fashion shown in the lower portion of Fig. 7. The experimenter encouraged the infant to play with the objects, employing such instructions as, "See these?—you play with them—you fix them all up!" The child's manipulations of the objects were observed behind a one-way mirror. If the infant failed to group the objects spontaneously, the experimenter raised the tray and provided recessed containers on either side. These are shown in the lower portion of Fig. 7 as dotted rectangles (Tasks II and IV) and dotted circles (Tasks I and III). The examiner, while pointing to the two containers in turn, suggested to the infant that he or she "put some here and some here."

Scoring of the infants' performance on the tasks described differed somewhat from procedures employed with slightly older children. In the latter case, observation has generally been confined to the grouping of the objects, that is, their spatial separation into groups. Although such object grouping was also scored in Ricciuti's work, that author also noted that the infants' behavior could be scored for temporal ordering, that is, the order in which the objects were manipulated or displaced. It was apparently not uncommon for infants to handle the objects in a systematic temporal order (for example, four large objects followed by four small objects) while failing to produce a consistent spatial grouping. A further refinement of the scoring system distinguished between completely "correct" and partially "correct" groupings and between grouping operations (temporal or spatial) carried out on both or on only one of the object sets.

The overall patterning of the results for both temporal and spatial ordering can be described most succinctly as an age x task interaction. In respect to selective temporal ordering, Task I yielded the highest level (67% of the infants); Tasks II and III, an intermediate level (45 and 44% of the infants, respectively); and Task IV, an exceedingly low level (12% of the infants). At the same time, the first three tasks produced positive slopes with age, but Task IV yielded highly similar outcomes for the 12-, 18-, and 24-month-old infants. The general trend in respect to complete versus partial and two-set versus one-set ordering suggests that the former in each case was more typical of the older infants, the latter more characteristic of the younger (although the Ns were much too small to permit definitive statistical comparisons).

The level of systematic object grouping, as one might expect, was less than the level of selective temporal ordering. The overall percentages for Tasks I, II, III, and IV were 50, 39, 21, and 14, respectively. A consistent positive slope with age was found only for Task I. It is important to note that the foregoing percentages were comprised largely of incomplete groupings and operations on one rather than both subsets of stimuli for the various tasks. None of the

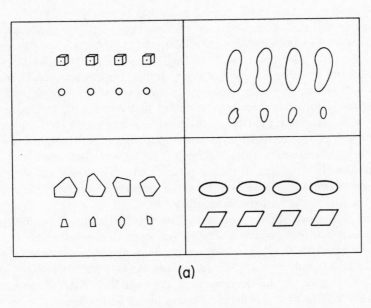

(a)

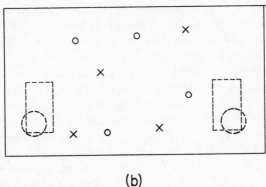

(b)

FIG. 7   (a) Schematic drawings of test objects: Task I, multiple–contrast; Task II, simple size–contrast; Task III, complex size–contrast; Task IV, form–contrast. (b) Standard arrangement for presentation (x indicates the locations of cubes, large object, and parallelograms). (From Ricciuti, 1965.)

12-month-olds and less than 15% of the 18- and 24-month-olds were able to make a complete and separate grouping of the two subsets within a task.

It is instructive to compare these latter data with Denney's (1972b) results for 2-year-olds (ranging from 2 years 2 months to 2 years 11 months). Of the 36 children in that age group, only two manifested complete similarity groupings. Of course, Denney's task seems more difficult (32 stimulus items that can be sorted by form, color, and size). Yet a single demonstration by an adult model was sufficient to induce complete similarity groupings spontaneously (Denney & Acito, 1974). One can only wonder, of course, as to how Ricciuti's 12- and 18-month-old infants would have responded to such a simple training effort. Of equal importance is the issue of the possible generalizability of such training to new sets of stimuli. There is good reason to believe that Ricciuti's research has not by any means tested the limits of the infant's classification prowess. Nevertheless, that research strongly suggests that there may be stimulus-induced cognitive organizations conducive to serial and spatial groupings in the absence of verbal or symbolic mediational processes.[6]

A major concern of this chapter is to trace the antecedents of cognitive styles as far back into infancy as is feasible. Where styles of conceptualization are at issue, we have observed that rudimentary grouping by similarity can be observed as early as 12 months of age. However, how can one articulate such findings with the observed stylistic preferences of later childhood? All of the infancy and early childhood research on grouping by similarity discussed so far has employed geometric forms as stimuli. Grouping by color, form, or size would be categorized as "descriptive-global" responses in the Sigel et al. (1967) scoring method, and as "analytic-descriptive" in the Kagan et al. (1963) method. Inhelder and Piaget's (1964) graphic collections (designs and constructions) involve complementary relations between stimuli and hence would be classified as "relational" or "relational-contextual" by the scoring methods cited above. As stage theorists, Inhelder and Piaget maintain that complementarity precedes similarity in the course of cognitive development, the latter eventually displacing the former in the child's cognitive repertoire. Denney (1972a), however, has raised doubts (not necessarily conclusive) about complementarity as a stage, and Denney and Acito (1974) have shown how very easily the similarity response can be acquired by children 2–3 years of age who spontaneously produced graphic or complementary patterns.[7] It would be very surprising indeed if training in the opposite direction—modeling complementarity for children who spontaneously group by similarity—were not equally successful. In short, if similarity and complementarity do not represent immediately available response options to the child as young as 2 years, it apparently requires little

[6]The possibility that classification by similarity may precede language development is a critical theoretical issue, but one that is tangential to the concerns of this book.

[7]In a recent publication, Denney (1974) partially retreats to a stage position, but she attributes the observed developmental changes primarily to environmental rather than organismic determinants.

effort to provide such children with the same kind of option available to children more advanced in age. The intriguing unknown in the present context is the lower age limit for the induction of the kinds of stylistic preferences described.

To a considerable degree, the distinction between a "stage" formulation and a stylistic-preference position has been too sharply drawn. A close reading of Inhelder and Piaget (1964) clearly indicates that the difference between graphic and nongraphic collections (complementarity versus similarity) is by no means sharp. Similarity relations often intrude on graphic collections. A simple change in the wording of instructions—"put together whatever is alike" versus "put together whatever goes together" directly influences the incidence of complementary and similarity groupings. "Alike" instructions enhance similarity grouping; "goes together" instructions enhance complementary grouping. Comparable results have been obtained with 6-year-olds on the Conceptual Styles Test (Stanes, 1973). In short, similarity relations are lacking in the groupings of very young children only if one insists on a performance criterion of hierarchical logical classification.

To what degree are the described outcomes restricted to geometric shapes? Inhelder and Piaget (1964) insist that similar findings ensue from the use of geometric shapes or real objects. Graphic designs are deemed analogous to relational-contextual groupings (for example, a baby is grouped with a cot instead of with other human figures). Both involve complementary relations between stimuli (see Denney, 1974). Nevertheless, it must be granted that geometric shapes are artificial stimuli bearing little relation to real objects in the child's environment; therefore, it would be highly informative to examine the grouping behavior of infants and very young children with materials having more of an experiential base. Such a study has been carried out by Katherine Nelson (1973b). Regrettably, the study can only be given "pilot" status, because it is based on a mere seven children, ranging in age from 19 to 22 months.

Nelson's basic hypothesis is that the dimension of greatest relevance to very young children in categorizing realistic objects is that of function—how the object is used in action. Even prior to 2 years of age, the child has had considerable experience with the ways objects "work," which necessarily implies that functional dimensions are in the cognitive repertoire of the child at an early age. This further implies that such strictly perceptual attributes as form, color, and size are secondary in the formation of categories. The difficulties in grouping experienced by the infants in the Ricciuti study now begin to make considerable sense, for these subjects, in the context of the experiment itself, had to learn perceptual distinctions having little primacy in their everyday lives. The categorizations already acquired by the infant were presumably of little value in the light of the abstract, nonmeaningful stimuli employed.

Nelson's experimental format was quite similar to that used by Ricciuti. The stimulus materials, however, were decidedly different. These included plastic models of cars, planes, animals, eating utensils, cylinders, and blocks.

Table 1 (from Nelson, 1973b) indicates the manner in which the stimuli were grouped, the basis of classification relevant to the grouping, and the order in which the groups were presented.

Despite the small sample size ($N = 7$), the results were strikingly suggestive of the primacy of function (and of function in combination with form and color) in the children's sequential choices. In each case, all of the tested children made sequential choices exceeding chance expectations. Size and color, in contrast, produced as much alternating as sequential behavior. The foregoing data were reasonably consistent with the outcomes for spatial grouping in the sense that all of the children in the function-form-color conditions and five of the seven children in the pure function condition produced spatial groups. At the same time, however, five of the seven children also formed spatial groups purely on the basis of form. Finally, color yielded lower levels of grouping, and none of the children grouped on the basis of size. This last finding runs counter to that reported by Ricciuti, who obtained a higher level of grouping for size than for form as a basis for classification. Nelson's and Ricciuti's results are quite consistent, however, in showing that very few children under 2 years of age operate on both subsets when forming spatial groups. Only 1 of the 7 children in

TABLE 1

Groups and Classification Basis
in Order of Presentation[a]

Group	Classification Basis
1. 4 Large blue plastic planes 4 Small blue plastic planes	Size
2. 4 Small green plastic animals (varied) 4 Small yellow plastic animals (varied)	Color
or	
4 Blue cars (varied) 4 Yellow cars (varied)	
3. 2 Blue cylinders 2 Blue blocks 2 Yellow cylinders 2 Yellow blocks	Color or form (and function)
4. 4 Small plastic green animals (varied) 4 Small plastic green eating utensils (varied)	Function
5. 4 Small yellow plastic cars (varied) 4 Small blue plastic planes (varied)	Color and form (and function)

[a]From Nelson (1973b).

Nelson's sample displaced four objects of each kind from their original location and constituted them as spatially separated groups.

Although the relative primacy of form, color, and size is left in doubt by the Ricciuti and Nelson investigations, the latter has rather clearly demonstrated that the function of objects is of critical relevance for classification behavior in children under 2 years of age. The two studies considered together suggest that categorization is so very basic a cognitive process as to occur before the child is capable of both comprehending instructions to classify and verbally explaining his basis for sequentially selecting and/or spatially grouping objects placed before him.[8] The commonly accepted view (e.g., Inhelder & Piaget, 1964; Denney, 1974) that very young children relate to objects strictly on the basis of complementarity (for example, graphic constructions) is clearly shown to be in error. Grouping behavior based on similarity can evidently be found in children as young as 12 months of age. There is little doubt, in other words, that a child possesses the capacity to categorize objects by adult criteria of similarity before he or she is able to name them.

Beyond the issue of the child's capacity to categorize by similarity, Nelson (1973b) has addressed herself to the criteria that the child employs in making such categorizations. In support of earlier research (Palmer & Rees, 1969), the 2-year-olds in Nelson's study demonstrated a greater mastery of the meaning of functional than of perceptual concepts. In the present context, "functional" refers to temporary states of objects (for example, empty, open, clean), whereas "perceptual" refers to the permanent attributes of objects (for example, smooth, black, soft). This implies that the very young child is more sensitive to within-things variability (temporary states) than to between-things variability (perceptual attributes of size, color, and shape). Many of the objects in the child's natural environment have the potential for change (for example, an empty bottle can be filled), and it is these changing states that seem to be more salient to the 2-year-old than are the object's permanent perceptual qualities.

Nelson (1973b) reports a further experiment on the relative dominance of form and function in the categorization of infants aged 15-20 months. Working with the "ball" concept, Nelson assembled a set of 27 objects varying in extent of their "ball-like" properties. These were then ranked by a group of adult judges independently along dimensions of form and function relative to the

---

[8]Categorization processes have been observed in infants as young as 1 month of age for speech perception (Eimas, Siqueland, Jusczyk, & Vigorito, 1971) and as young as 4 months of age for color (hue) perception (Bornstein, Kessen, & Weiskopf, 1976). Such findings reinforce the view that categorical perception, instead of being learned, may well be part of the biological endowment of the individual (see also Lenneberg, 1967). Other research by Bornstein (1975) on color perception in young infants has demonstrated differential fixation time to focal and boundary hues, the former being looked at longer. Although such fixation times seem to be related to adult color preferences, within-infant differences between focal and boundary fixation times may represent an early analog of breadth versus narrowness of categorization.

prototypical child's rubber ball. Three objects were then selected for each of three categories—those most like the ball in function but unlike in form; those most like the ball in form but unlike in function; those most unlike the ball in form and function. These nine objects (plus a child's rubber ball included as a standard) were arranged in front of the child. The experimenter asked the child to give her the ball. The child's choice was removed from the group and the process repeated until five choices had been made. These objects were then returned to the group, and 10 min of free play with the various objects was encouraged. Following this period, the objects were again aligned before the child and five successive choices again obtained to the experimenter's request that the child give her the ball.

The results of the foregoing study revealed a significant pre- to posttest shift in choice of objects. Prior to the period of free exploratory play, the children's choices were equiprobable in respect to form and function. Following the play period, however, a significant shift to choices based on function was observed. Although these findings emphasize the salience of function in categorizing by children under 2 years of age, it is of interest nevertheless that the choices were evenly divided in the pretest between form and function. Whether this represents a meaningful individual-difference dimension in children under 2 years old is moot, for Nelson has not ordered her data in that manner. The data do suggest, however, that children do store information about typical form and use it in categorizing new instances. In Nelson's view, the very young child "forms categories on the basis of function and generalizes to new instances on the basis of form [p. 33]."

How can one proceed to reconcile the outcomes of the Nelson study with evidence based on older children indicating a developmental shift from perceptual to functional bases for grouping of objects (e.g., Bruner et al., 1966). In Nelson's opinion, the discrepancy is more apparent than real, for both functional and perceptual bases for grouping can vary dramatically in level of complexity. In other words, the perceptual and functional attributes employed by the 18 month old and the 8 year old will assume characteristic age-appropriate forms. Functional groupings will become less concrete and more abstract, and perceptual groupings will become less global and more analytic. It is clearly in error, then, to conceive of unilinear cognitive development proceeding from the perceptual to the functional. As Werner (1957) asserted many years ago, development proceeds in multilinear fashion, implying that perceptual and functional modes of conceptualizing exist side by side in the child's repertoire with both becoming more differentiated and complex during the course of development (see also Kagan & Kogan, 1970, pp. 1284-1285).

The evidence in favor of multilinear development, however, does not settle the issue of origins. Are the infant's earliest concepts formed on a perceptual or functional basis? This question has generated some controversy between Clark (1973), who favors a perceptual interpretation, and Nelson (1974b), who has argued for the predominance of the functional aspect in early concept and word acquisition.

Clark offers a "semantic features" hypothesis according to which the child's earliest words are based on one or two features (customarily perceptual in character) in contrast to the multiple features typical of adult word meanings. Clark cites as an example the word "dog," where the child's meaning may focus exclusively on "four leggedness." This implies that the young child overextends the concept and that it is only with the acquisition of the other semantic features that the concept is progressively narrowed down until the full adult meaning is attained. The supporting evidence that Clark offers for the early perceptual overextensions and subsequent narrowing down derives largely from available diaries devoted to the early speech of children ranging from approximately 1 to 2½ years of age. Overextensions are described that are based on movement, shape, size, sound, taste, and texture.

Limitations of the "overextension" interpretation were considered in the previous chapter in the context of breadth of categorization. Here, the emphasis is necessarily placed on the adequacy of the view that the child's earliest concepts derive from the perceptual comparison of exemplars. Nelson (1974b) offers the most compelling argument against the foregoing hypothesis. Only a portion of that argument is discussed here, for the issues extend well beyond the concerns of this chapter (and volume) into the matter of the nature of the linkages between early concept and language acquisition. In Nelson's view, the abstraction of criterial perceptual attributes from a set of exemplars represents a later phase of the concept-formation process. The earliest phase is a within-object rather than a between-object matter, the infant interacting with a particular object as a whole in dyanamic action contexts. For example, a first ball will be experienced in a context of place (for example, porch), agent of action (for example, mother), nature of action (for example, throws), and effects of action (for example, bounces). Some of these may change when a second ball is encountered (for example, thrown by a sibling outdoors). Whereas all of these contextual aspects may initially be retained within the "ball" concept, the child eventually recognizes that some relationships constitute a functional core (for example, rolls, bounces). At this stage, then, new instances of the concept are identified to the degree that they share the dynamic action possibilities represented in the functional core. It is important to note that no perceptual analysis whatever has been brought into play up to this point. At a later point, of course, the child will want to be able to pick out a ball from among other objects outside of an action context. Perceptual attributes assume a high degree of relevance at this juncture, and it can be expected that "roundness" in due course proves to be criterial. Therefore, Nelson views concept formation as initially a synthesizing process–the building up of a functional core in a dynamic action context. The subsequent perceptual-analytic phase (essentially secondary) is presumed to follow directly after a concept is formed.

On the whole, Nelson (1974b) presents an extremely persuasive case for the primacy of the functional mode in the infant's earliest conceptualizations. One must not forget, however, that the temporal sequence proposed—functional as primary, perceptual-analytic as secondary—although highly compelling, remains an hypothesis in need of confirmation. Nelson's (1973b) preliminary experimental work is only partially supportive of the hypothesis. In fact, those results (discussed earlier) are not inconsistent with the view that the functional and perceptual modes are employed simultaneously rather than sequentially in the infant's initial concept acquisitions.[9]

C. VALIDATION AT THE PRESCHOOL LEVEL

1. Relation to Socioemotional and Task-Oriented Behaviors in Five-Year-Olds

Published empirical studies relating styles of conceptualization to behavioral information in preschool children are very scarce. Indeed, I have been able to locate only one such study (Sigel *et al.*, 1967). Middle-class 4- and 5-year-old boys and girls were administered the modified version of the 20-item triads task described earlier. It will be recalled that each triad of pictures was accompanied by a fourth item as a standard, the child being given the task of selecting one of the pictures in the triad that "is like or goes with" the standard (see Fig. 6). In the present version, the scoring categories were descriptive part-whole, descriptive-global, relational-contextual, and categorical-inferential. The child's personal-social behavior was assessed by the children's nursery-school teachers, using an 11-item set of 10-point rating scales devised by Davidson and Sarason (1961). Two teachers rated each child independently with a high degree of agreement.

Correlations obtained between the teacher ratings and the styles of conceptualization (reported only for the 5 year olds) were markedly different for boys and girls. In the case of the boys, higher scores on descriptive part-whole conceptualizing were significantly associated with higher ratings on a "controls emotion" scale. Girls inclined toward descriptive part-whole conceptualizing, in contrast, were rated by their teachers as not cautious, tending to daydream, and inattentive. In respect to relational-contextual conceptualizing, boys inclined in that direction were rated as low on "controls emotion," whereas a

[9]Farnham-Diggory and Gregg (1975) attempt to resolve the Clark-Nelson controversy by maintaining that the perceptual and functional represent different microgenetic stages of the classification process. It is dubious whether such a resolution captures the essence of the issue for very young children in the early concept-formation period. Farnham-Diggory and Gregg (whose research is based on 5 year olds and adults) are reasoning for a later developmental stage when both functional and perceptual options are available to the child.

slight trend in the opposite direction was observed for girls. Descriptive-global and categorical-inferential conceptualizing also yielded different patterns of correlations with teacher ratings for boys and girls, but the psychological significance of the differences is less clear.

In sum, the findings clearly point to sex as a strong moderator variable in respect to the cognition-behavior linkage in preschool children. Indeed, Maccoby (1966) employs the data of Sigel *et al.* (1967) to illustrate the viability of her curvilinear model for explaining sex differences in cognition-behavior relationships. The model rests on the implicit assumption that boys exceed girls on a hypothetical dimension of boldness and/or impulsiveness. In order for that model to apply, one must accept the value judgment that the descriptive part-whole approach is superior to relational-contextual conceptualizing. The model would also have to assume that teachers rated girls higher than boys on caution and attentiveness. Regrettably, Sigel *et al.* (1967) did not report these data in their published article.[10]

2. Relation to Socioemotional and Task-Oriented Behaviors in Three- and Four-Year-Olds

The study described above is based on a relatively small sample of 48 5-year-old children. The reported sex differences are quite dramatic, but it is doubtful whether they should be given full-fledged acceptance without replication. The Block and Block project, as indicated earlier, offers measures of conceptualizing styles from Sigel's Object Categorization Test as well as teacher *Q*-sort ratings. Although the available findings are based on younger children (3- and 4-year-olds) and on a different cognitive task (the SOCT rather than a triads task), it would nevertheless be of some interest to observe whether any consistencies can be found.

Block and Block have analyzed their data separately for 3- and 4-year-olds. The number of subjects was 38 boys and 52 girls for the 3-year-olds, and 53 boys and 59 girls for the 4-year-olds. The most powerful generalizations that can be drawn from the data concern the striking sex and age differences in the correlations obtained. The former is consistent with the general outcomes reported by Sigel *et al.* (1967), and the latter enormously complicates interpretation of results. It appears that styles of conceptualization do not have similar behavioral implications over the age span of 3-5 years, nor are these implications consistent across sex within a particular age group.

   a. The descriptive and relational-contextual modes in boys. Consider first the index of descriptive conceptualizing derived from the SOCT. The overall

[10]Other data collected and summarized by Maccoby and Jacklin (1974) do not support the presence of the sex difference indicated.

picture for the high-descriptive 3-year-old boy is strongly suggestive of high-resilient overcontrol (Block & Block, 1973). Teachers described these children as responsive to reason, attentive, planful, and reflective—all characteristics that are reasonably consistent with the "emotional control" reported by Sigel et al. (1967) for high-descriptive (part-whole) 5-year-old boys. However, the Blocks also found that their 3-year-old high-descriptive boys were characterized as having unusual thought processes, strong involvements in tasks, and a creative approach in "perception, thought, work, or play." These qualities are not suggestive of overcontrol. Because these boys were also rated as being of high intellectual capacity, one comes away with an impression of children distinguished by an all-pervasive cognitive strength in no way hampered by emotional difficulties or interferences.

It will be recalled that the Blocks found no stability in conceptualizing styles for boys across the age span of 3-4 years. Hence, it is no great surprise to discover that all of the virtues associated with the descriptive style at age 3 years have essentially disappeared at 4 years of age, without any other compensating virtues emerging. Indeed, the 4-year-old high-descriptive boy is described as "restless and fidgety," "indecisive and vacillating." In respect to the relational-contextual style for 3- and 4-year-old boys, the pattern is basically the converse of that reported for the descriptive style. The negative behavioral implications of the relational style at age 3 years have disappeared by age 4 years. It is hard to know what to make of such dramatic change over a 1-year period. If the Blocks' results for ages 3 and 4 years had been reversed, one might have been able to discern a pattern of continuity with the 5-year-olds studied by Sigel et al. (1967) and the older children and adults investigated by Kagan and his associates (Kagan et al., 1963, 1964). Instead, we are confronted with a puzzling discontinuity the psychological meaning of which remains obscure.

b.   The descriptive and relational-contextual modes in girls.   Consider next the Block and Block findings for the girls. In the case of the 3-year-olds, high descriptiveness was associated with a set of positively toned characteristics. Whereas the strengths of the 3-year-old descriptive boys seemed to emerge in the cognitive area, however, the strengths of their female counterparts clearly appeared in the social area. These girls were rated highly on considerateness, and they were described as getting "along well with other children," developing "genuine and close relationships," being "admired and sought out," and tending "to give, lend, and share." They were judged as able to "delay gratification," unaggressive, and not easily irritated. It can be readily seen that these qualities bear little resemblance to the impulsivity and inattentiveness observed in 5-year-old high-descriptive girls by Sigel et al. (1967). Once again, however, the picture changed quite dramatically at age 4 years, as the high-descriptive girls now yielded marginal negative relationships with the social virtues described above and significant positive relationships with such behaviors as attempting to "transfer blame to others" and to "stretch limits," expressing "negative feelings directly and openly," not giving in "when in conflict with others," and being noncompliant and stubborn.

In sum, certain aspects of the uninhibitedness and impulsivity of the 5-year-old-descriptive girls observed by Sigel *et al.* (1967) can be discerned in the 4-year-old girls studied by the Blocks. In this respect, the data for the girls are distinguished by a modicum of continuity that is markedly lacking in the boys. This continuity seems to extend to the relational-contextual style as well, for no clear-cut pattern of relationships with the Q-sort items emerged in either the 3- or the 4-year-old girls. It will be recalled that Sigel *et al.* (1967) also failed to obtain any behavioral correlates of a relational-contextual style in 5-year-old girls.

c. The categorical-inferential mode in boys.   Although the categorical-inferential mode of conceptualization has received sketchy theoretical treatment at the hands of Kagan and Sigel and their associates, the findings for that style obtained by the Blocks are reported here for the sake of completeness. One cannot afford to forget that the styles of conceptualization are ipsatively scored, implying that positive relationships for one of the styles generates the statistical likelihood of negative relationships with one of the remaining two. With three alternatives, of course, it is not possible to predict the patterning of the relationships in advance. The direction of this patterning can vary and hence affords still another opportunity for the emergence of sex and age differences.

For the 3-year-old boys, categorical-inferential conceptualizing had virtually no behavioral correlates. In that age and sex group, then, the distinction between the descriptive and relational-contextual styles was crucial in respect to behavioral validation. By 4 years of age, it will be recalled, the latter styles had lost their predictive utility in boys. It is the categorical-inferential style that generated behavioral correlates in boys 4 years of age. Teachers judged these high categorical-inferential boys to have high intellectual capacity. Most salient, however, were the socioemotional qualities attributed to these children. They were described as aggressive, self-assertive, noncompliant, judgmental, distrustful, inconsiderate, and ready to take advantage of other children. In short, teachers acknowledged the intellectual strength of these children but at the same time attributed a broad array of antisocial tendencies.

d. The categorical-inferential mode in girls.   The behavioral implications of the categorical-inferential style in the girls concern us next. It will be recalled that the behavioral correlates of the descriptive style in the girls changed from a syndrome of qualities indicative of prosocial tendencies and emotional control at 3 years of age to the very opposite pattern at 4 years of age. The relational-contextual style proved to have little behavioral relevance for the girls. The Q-sort correlates of high categorical-inferential conceptualizing in 3-year-old girls formed a pattern of low-resilient undercontrol (Block & Block, 1973). This pattern—a combination of antisocial dispositions and low emotional control—reversed itself at 4 years of age to yield a picture of high-resilient overcontrol. Prosocial dispositions and high emotional control appeared to characterize the high categorical-inferential 4-year-old girl.

   e.   Summary and interpretation.   It is evident, then, that the distinction between descriptive and categorical-inferential conceptualizing is critical in respect to contrasting behaviors for girls. The relational-contextual mode carries little weight. For the boys, in contrast, the descriptive versus relational-contextual contrast is of behavioral relevance at 3 years of age, but that dichotomy loses its predictive power at 4 years of age. The categorical-inferential style carries the behavioral freight for boys at that age.

   Given the complexity of these outcomes, a brief summary would seem to be in order. At 3 years of age, descriptive conceptualizing had positive behavioral implications for both boys and girls—largely in the cognitive domain for the former and in the socioemotional domain for the latter. The contrasting poles of that stylistic dimension at 3 years of age were relational-contextual conceptualizing for boys and categorical-inferential conceptualizing for girls. By 4 years of age, the overall picture has changed quite dramatically. In the case of the boys, the descriptive versus relational-contextual contrast has ceased to have much behavioral relevance. The categorical-inferential style has come to the fore, with boys high on the dimension characterized by a syndrome of self-assertive, dominant, aggressive, and antisocial behavior (although within a context of judged high intellectual capacity). For girls, in contrast, the descriptive versus categorical-inferential contrast continued to have behavioral significance, but the psychological meaning assigned to the poles was essentially reversed between the ages of 3 and 4 years. At the latter age, the descriptive and categorical-inferential styles had negative and positive socioemotional implications, respectively. This reversal occurred in spite of the relative stability of the two styles in the girls between 3 and 4 years of age.

   What is one to make of the foregoing pattern of outcomes? One particularly striking finding is the degree to which the styles of conceptualization are associated with both socioemotional and cognitively oriented behaviors in the case of the boys, but only with the former in the case of the girls. Whether this represents a genuinely greater separation between the socioemotional and cognitive behavioral domains for girls than for boys or sex-role stereotypes in the implicit personality theory of the nursery-school teachers cannot be determined from the Blocks' data. The issue is certainly worthy of further investigation.

   One possible avenue along which interpretation of the shifting age and sex effects may be feasible has been called the style versus capacity distinction (e.g., Wachtel, 1968). It is essentially a developmental idea in which cognitive functions with the characteristic of a stylistic preference at later ages assume the qualities of a capacity at earlier ages. In other words, the younger child may recognize only one way to respond on the SOCT, whereas the older child may be aware of alternative possibilies.[11] One may be stretching a point to apply the foregoing scheme to the age period of 3-4 years, but it is surely worth the effort in the absence of other compelling options.

For 3-year-old boys, the relational-contextual mode probably represents a developmentally immature response. It is reflective of complementarity as opposed to similarity (Denney, 1974) and more than likely signifies that the child has not yet reached the stage of grouping spontaneously by similarity. Hence, it is not too surprising that nursery-school teachers produce Q sorts for these children that are suggestive of cognitive immaturity and weakness. The descriptive style, in contrast, indicates that the child is capable of grouping by similarity and, as we have seen, the high-descriptive 3-year-old boy is rated highly by his teachers on a wide variety of positive cognitive characteristics. By the time the male child has attained the age of 4 years, however, the mere ability to group by similarity is likely to have lost much of its earlier predictive significance, because it is now in the repertoire of most middle-class children of that age. Hence, the decline in the behavioral validity of the descriptive mode makes a certain amount of sense. At this age, it is the categorical-inferential mode that is likely to be more atypical and subtle and, as we have noted, that mode is associated with teacher ratings of high intellectual capacity. The self-assertiveness, aggressiveness, and dominance also typical of these children may well represent part of a broader syndrome of testing one's emerging intellectual powers in a variety of contexts (including an object-sorting task). Such testing of one's social environment may well have disruptive effects, and it may account for the attribution of antisocial tendencies to the high categorical-inferential 4-year-old boys.

It is considerably more difficult to arrive at so coherent an explanation for the girls. If one presumes that preschool boys lag behind preschool girls by approximately 1 year on a hypothetical "developmental maturity" dimension (a presumption that receives reasonable empirical support in research reviewed earlier), the interpretive path is somewhat eased. If 3-year-old girls have been capable of grouping by similarity for some time, the relational-contextual mode can be expected to have lesser behavioral import than is the case in boys of the same age. The Block and Block data are consistent with the foregoing inference. At the same time, the mere fact that 3-year-old girls can group by similarity is not as outstanding an accomplishment for these girls relative to boys of the same age. The evidence that high-descriptive 3-year-old girls exhibit consistent prosocial behaviors simply informs us that these girls have been well-socialized to the prevalent female sex-role stereotype. However, the 3-year-old girls who preferred and/or were capable of categorical-inferential conceptualizing (possibly

[11]It is acknowledged that the younger child can be easily trained to entertain other alternatives, although he may have only one alternative available when confronting the task for the first time (see Denney & Acito, 1974).

the more sophisticated similarity response) appear to be in rebellion against the stereotypical prosocial pattern. Interestingly enough, the teachers did not attribute to these girls any of the compensating virtues (such as high intellectual capacity) that were assigned to the high categorical-inferential 4-year-old boy.

Why does the pattern of behavioral correlates for the 4-year-old girls reverse itself relative to the findings for girls 1 year younger? This is the most difficult question of all. The shift in the meaning of the descriptive mode from prosocial (with high emotional control) at age 3 years to antisocial (with low emotional control) at age 4 years strongly suggests that a close look at the descriptive index is warranted. It will be recalled that the index combines what had formerly been separated—global and part-whole responses. Is it possible that the former is more typical at 3 years of age and the latter more frequent at 4 years of age? Such a shift would make good developmental sense and would furthermore render the data for the 4-year-old girls consistent with the Sigel et al. (1967) results for girls 5 years of age. In respect to the switch in the categorical-inferential response, it should be noted that Sigel et al. (1967) obtained near significant positive relationships between categorical-inferential conceptualizing and "communicability" in 5-year-old girls. Hence, the prosocial qualities of the 4-year-old high categorical-inferential girls observed by the Blocks represents further evidence in favor of continuity.

In sum, it appears that, at least for the present, we shall have to accept the view that the behavioral implications of conceptualizing styles change quite radically as the middle-class child matures from ages 3 to 4 years. At the same time, a searching look at the Sigel indices is clearly required. A variety of responses may possess the formal properties deemed necessary for inclusion under one of the three conceptualizing styles. Yet these responses may vary considerably in level of sophistication or complexity and hence have different implications for other aspects of the child's functioning. It will be granted that Sigel's scoring manual for the SOCT includes an overall accuracy score (considered earlier in connection with breadth of categorization). There is much to recommend the use of separate accuracy or quality components for each of the styles, however. The use of such scores alongside the traditional style indices might go a long way toward explicating many of the puzzling age and sex effects distinguishing this cognitive-style domain.

D.   PARENTAL INFLUENCES

Two studies have appeared exploring the influence of parents on the preschool child's style of conceptualizing. The first of these (Hess & Shipman, 1965) examined the relationship between the conceptualizing styles of mother and child. The Hess-Shipman research was based on a sample of 163 black mothers and their 4-year-old children. These were approximately equally divided across four levels of social status—college-educated professionals, high-school-educated skilled blue collar, elementary-school-educated semi- or unskilled, and father-absent welfare cases. All of the mothers were given a conceptual-style task intended for adults—the MAPS task (Kagan *et al.*, 1963). This procedure requires the subject to make 12 consecutive sorts from a highly diversified set of human figure drawings. As in the case of the conceptual-style tasks intended for children, the MAPS is scored for the number of descriptive, relational-contextual, and categorical-inferential groupings. The children in the Hess-Shipman study were given the Sigel task described earlier (Sigel *et al.*, 1967), consisting of triads of pictures and a fourth picture to be grouped with one member of the triad.

The social status of the mothers influenced MAPS performance—descriptive and categorical-inferential sorts linked positively to social status and relational-contextual sorts negatively associated with social status. In respect to the performance of the children, nonscorable responses predominated and increased as social status declined. Where scorable responses were obtained, the incidence of all three styles of conceptualization—descriptive, relational-contextual, and categorical-inferential—declined with decreasing social status. Hess and Shipman reported that a positive correlation was obtained between the mother's use of relational-contextual responses and the child's emission of nonscorable responses. Regrettably, the size of that correlation is not reported.

On the basis of their findings, Hess and Shipman strongly endorse the original position of Kagan and his associates (Kagan *et al.*, 1963; Kagan *et al.*, 1964) concerning the cognitive immaturity of the relational-contextual style. This style was more characteristic of lower than of higher status mothers, and it was the children of the former group who performed poorly on the Sigel sorting task. What are the mediating mechanisms, however? Hess and Shipman favor Bernstein's (1961) view of the close link between social class and restricted versus elaborated linguistic codes. Lower-class mothers in teaching their children are presumed to use restricted, status- and punishment-oriented codes and commands. One might expect that such a teaching style would be highly discouraging of the rational mastery of cognitive tasks on the part of the preschool child.

Although the Hess and Shipman study breaks new ground in its demonstration of linkages between conceptual styles of mothers and their children, the research suffers from a number of shortcomings that detract from the conclusions drawn. No statistical tests are employed, and hence it is difficult to interpret the mean differences in conceptual styles (often slight) across the four social-status groups. One particularly misses a table of correlations relating the styles of mothers and children. Finally, the interpretations regarding mediating processes would have been more convincing if the actual empirical relationships between the conceptual style variables and the mother's style of teaching her child had been obtained.[12]

Some of the foregoing difficulties are overcome in a study carried out by Davis and Lange (1973), although those authors did not work with the social-class variable. All subjects (18 parent couples and their children) were middle class. Fathers as well as mothers were included in the study. The children ranged in age from 4 to 5 years.

All of the children were given the same Sigel *et al.* (1967) sorting task that had been used by Hess and Shipman (1965). Several weeks after this administration, each parent, independent of spouse, was invited to spend an hour interacting with his or her child. The interaction focused on two tasks—storytelling and block sorting. For the former, the parent was requested to tell the child a "bedtime" type of story to two animal pictures; for the latter, the parent was instructed to teach the child a block-sorting task where the attributes for sorting were shape, shade, height, and marking. Interaction between the parent and child was recorded, and the parents' verbal communications were converted into message units to be coded as descriptive, relational-contextual, and categorical-inferential. Interrater reliability of such coding was quite high (92% agreement).

The parents' linguistic styles varied significantly across the two tasks—more descriptive utterances for block sorting and more categorical-inferential utterances for storytelling. These differences are not surprising, for one would expect a block-sorting task to force a concentration on manifest perceptual properties of the stimuli, whereas storytelling would be more likely to emphasize the inferred characteristics of stimuli. The outcomes of major importance concern the relationship between the parents' linguistic style and the child's conceptual style. Correlations carried out for mothers and fathers separately did not yield much of interest. When the data were averaged by parent couple, however, significant correlations were obtained between the parents' incidence of descriptive communications and the child's preference for the descriptive style on the Sigel task in the case of both storytelling ($r = .46$) and block sorting ($r = .41$). No significant relationships were found for the other two styles.

Although the Davis and Lange (1973) research represents a genuine breakthrough in respect to demonstrating a homologous relation between the linguistic style of the parents and the preferred conceptual style of the child, the work cannot help but raise further questions. It is not entirely clear, for example, why the relationship should emerge exclusively in the descriptive domain. The indication that the data for mothers and fathers must be combined to yield a positive outcome points to the relative independence of linguistic

[12]Most of these methodological deficiencies have been remedied in a subsequent publication by Hess and Shipman (1967) concerned with maternal influences on cognitive functioning, but that paper focuses on ability rather than stylistic dimensions.

styles within parent couples—a mildly surprising finding. An obvious further analysis is suggested by the foregoing pattern. Parental couples evidently vary in the degree to which the mother and father resemble one another in linguistic style. The extent of this similarity-dissimilarity, in other words, might well be a major "moderator" variable. A reasonable hypothesis is that the stylistic match between parent and offspring increases systematically as parental linguistic styles become less dissimilar and more similar.

E. CONCLUSIONS AND IMPLICATIONS

The present cognitive domain can be distinguished from those previously discussed in several respects. Field independence-dependence, reflection-impulsivity, and breadth of categorization represent relatively new constructs in the science of psychology. All three have emerged on the scene subsequent to World War II, and one cannot point to any obvious historical antecedents in the earlier psychological literature.[13] In striking contrast, styles of conceptualization represent nothing more than a new way of looking at an old problem. In the simplest of terms, the problem is one of discovering and delineating the bases on which individuals decide that two or more nonidentical objects are similar to one another. The study of concept attainment and concept formation bears on this issue, as do the well-worn (pre-World War II) constructs of abstraction-concreteness and stimulus generalization (see Pikas, 1966). New labels have been coined to describe the phenomena of interest, but the fundamental questions have not changed too much. Concept attainment continues as a major topic within experimental psychology. At the same time, shifts in emphasis can be noted as investigators inquire into the bases for individual differences and ontogenetic changes in the grouping or sorting of objects.

A second distinction between the present cognitive-style domain and those considered earlier has methodological overtones. For each of the cognitive styles treated previously, both individual differences within age and developmental change from the preschool period onward are defined quantitatively on the basis of variation along polar dimensions. Just as children of a particular age vary in their proximity to one or the other pole of a specified dimension, so is each pole designated as the developmentally more and less "mature" mode in the expectation that older children fall closer to the more "mature" extreme and younger children to the less "mature" end of the dimension. It should be noted that the initial approach to each of the three styles cited has stressed individual differences among adults or children. Only later were age differences to fall within the purview of these researches, the underlying assumption being one of

---

[13]This is not to imply an absence of measurement antecedents. The EFT, for example, is directly derived from the Gottschaldt figures.

continuity and consistency across age. The older child is simply presumed to have more of a particular characteristic than does the younger child.

It would not be extreme to assert that the foregoing investigators deal in "forced opposites." If a child solves EFT problems readily, field independence is inferred. The opposite pole—field dependence—is inferred on the basis of poor EFT performance, not from a qualitatively distinctive performance of another kind. Similarly, if a child is slow in responding to MFF items, he or she cannot be fast at the same time. Making many errors on the MFF precludes making few errors. Correspondingly, broad categorizing necessarily rules out narrow categorizing.

The kinds of contrasts described lie at the core of psychological measurement and assessment within the individual-differences tradition. An alternative model is offered by the cognitive developmentalist, for whom age changes reflect qualitative shifts. The older child does not necessarily possess more of a particular attribute relative to the younger child; instead, the two exhibit different modes of cognitive functioning. It is typically assumed that earlier modes are abandoned as the child moves on to more mature levels of cognitive functioning. Despite the insistence on qualitative change, however, it is interesting to observe how variation in performance is typically dimensionalized to yield such polar contrasts as complementarity versus similarity or analytic versus nonanalytic. Where three modes are retained, as in much of the research of Kagan, Sigel, and their associates, an ipsative structure is maintained so that choice of a particular style necessarily reduces the manifestation of the remaining two.

As research on styles of conceptualization has proceeded, their preferential character has become strikingly apparent. Indeed, it is questionable whether earlier modes of conceptualizing are ever actually abandoned in favor of presumedly more advanced modes. Instead, for children as young as 2 years of age, alternative modes of conceptualizing may exist side by side in the child's cognitive repertoire, the particular mode chosen depending on the nature of the provided stimulus array and the general instructions to the task. This relativity of conceptual functioning was discussed in the earlier reviews (Kagan & Kogan, 1970; Kogan, 1971), and the subsequent accumulated evidence reported here for younger children does not seem to contradict it.

The prevalence of stylistic preferences in young children should not be taken to imply that capacities are of no importance in the conceptualizing domain. The problem for the future is to disentangle the stylistic and capacity components of conceptual functioning in children. It is likely that the capacity component assumes greater salience as one moves downward in age toward infancy. At the same time, we shall probably find that stylistic preference plays a role in the child's conceptualizations at quite an early age.

It is quite puzzling how investigators, on the whole, have failed to explore the young child's conceptual repertoire, even though such data can be obtained without detracting from the assessment of the preferential dimension. In the typical triads format, it is a simple additional step to ask the child, after the first preferred pairing, whether any other pairings are possible. Davis (1971) is one of few investigators to employ that procedure, and his data do not show the developmental trends reported by others. Exhausting the child's repertoire also enables the investigator to distinguish between preferences and capacities in the child's performance. The ease with which styles of conceptualization can be modified through training (e.g., D. R. Denney, 1972) strongly suggests that the newly taught style already has been in the child's repertoire prior to the training.

Preferences, of course, are highly malleable. They can be strikingly altered by training but they can be expected to change over time in the absence of deliberate modification efforts. The dramatic changes over a 1-year period observed by the Blocks in the cognitive and socioemotional correlates of the Sigel style measures testifies to the rapidly changing psychological significance of presumptively identical styles over relatively brief time periods. A stylistic choice deemed especially elegant at a particular point in time may lose much of its attractiveness as development proceeds. This does not mean that the former has dropped out of the child's repertoire. It may well reemerge at a still later point in development, but in more sophisticated form.

The time would appear to be ripe for a reorientation of research on styles of conceptualization. Let us determine not only what the child prefers to do, but what he is capable of doing. Let us depart from a rigidly unilinear model in which styles more and less mature follow one another according to a developmental timetable. Instead, let us plumb the repertoires of our subjects, recognizing that all of the styles may be present simultaneously (although possibly differing in their level of sophistication). Consistent with a multilinear model of development (Werner, 1957), let us explore the balance and patterning of styles within individuals. There may be more to the study of cognitive styles than traditional interindividual differences. Indeed, in its original meaning, the cognitive-style concept referred to the patterning of cognitive dimensions within persons (Klein, 1970). This early usage has essentially been ignored in recent work, and the study of styles of conceptualization is poorer for it.

VI

Interrelationships between Styles

Four cognitive styles have been critically examined in respect to assessment and validation in preschool children. In this chapter, we shall ask whether field dependence-independence, reflection-impulsivity, breadth of categorization, and styles of conceptualization bear any relation to one another at the preschool level.

A. TYPE I COGNITIVE STYLES

Where Type I cognitive styles are at issue—those based on veridicality of performance—positive relationships may be expected by virtue of common linkages to IQ. Are field dependence-independence and reflection-impulsivity positively associated, that is, are field-independent preschoolers more likely to be reflective and field dependents more likely to be impulsive? Banta (1970) reports a highly significant r of .49 between the foregoing two styles (MFF errors only) in the predicted direction in a sample of approximately 80 black lower class children. Unfortunately, these children ranged in age from 3 to 6 years, and because both field independence and reflection are known to increase with age, the reported correlation can be attributed directly to the age variable.

Banta's measures of reflection-impulsivity (EC-MFF) and field independence-dependence have also been employed by other investigators. In a sample of 73 disadvantaged preschoolers ranging from 35 to 59 months of age, Massari and Massari (1973) obtained highly significant correlations between EC-MFF errors and EC-EFT scores (−.45 and −.46, for boys and girls respectively). Once again, however, these significant relationships can be accounted for on the basis of the chronological age variable, given the 24-month age spread in the sample. Schleifer and Douglas (1973) administered Banta's tasks to samples of 35 middle-class and 37 disadvantaged preschoolers. Identical highly significant correlations of −.62 were obtained in both samples, but it should be noted that the age range was 41-71 months and 38-72 months in the middle-class and disadvantaged samples, respectively. It would be quite astonishing to discover that chronological age was not mediating the observed relationships given the age spreads of 30 and 34 months represented in the Schleifer and Douglas data.

Other relevant studies have been conducted in which the age range in the samples has been relatively narrow. For example, Mumbauer and Miller (1970) worked with samples of 32 middle-class and 32 disadvantaged preschoolers ranging in age from 56 to 68 months. A significant negative correlation of −.56 between MFF errors and CEFT is reported based on the combined samples. Because a marked intelligence difference would be anticipated between two such decidedly different samples, it would be very surprising indeed if an intelligence control did not result in a marked reduction in the magnitude of the foregoing correlation. In the case of the ETS Longitudinal Study (Shipman, 1972), factor analytic (rather than correlational) outcomes are reported. For 4 and 5 year olds, respectively, the first varimax factor yielded substantial loadings for the PEFT (.49 and .49), MFF errors (−.59 and −.65), motor inhibition (.42 and .44), and number of grouping responses on Sigel's Object Categorization Test—a general index of the child's capacity to understand and perform the task (.43 and .49). Note, however, that PPVT IQ also yielded fairly high loadings (.62 and .68), possibly reflecting the broad SES range of the ETS samples. Note further that MFF response time did not load on the foregoing factor but loaded on a second factor containing other latency measures. This finding parallels results reported by Massari and Massari (1973) indicating that EC-MFF response time is significantly related to EC-EFT response time (rs of .35 and .46 for boys and girls, respectively) but not to EC-EFT scores (rs of .26 and .20 for boys and girls, respectively).

The unpublished Block and Block findings did not fall into as coherent a pattern as that observed above. Comparisons are difficult, however, for Shipman (1972) does not report correlations, and the Blocks have not as yet applied factor analysis to their correlational outcomes. At the 3-year-old level, PEFT was significantly related to MFF errors in both boys and girls (rs of −.30 and −.31 respectively). Both of these dimensions were also related to PPVT IQ scores, but only marginally for PEFT (rs of .18 for boys and .17 for girls), although significantly for MFF errors (rs of −.34 for boys and −.39 for girls). MFF response time did not share in the foregoing relationship with IQ, an outcome that is consistent with both the Shipman (1972) and the Massari and Massari (1973) data. As one might expect, the accuracy measure from the SOCT also related significantly to IQ for both 3-year-old boys ($r = .40$) and girls ($r = .32$), but SOCT accuracy did not relate to PEFT or MFF scores. In sum, the results for the 3-year-olds are reasonably consistent in showing how Type I cognitive styles are linked to IQ in 3-year-olds, although the generality across these styles was far from perfect.

Some attenuation of the foregoing outcomes occurred in the sample of 4-year-olds. For example, the significant correlation between PEFT and MFF errors has essentially disappeared, yet each in turn remained modestly associated with IQ (WPPSI and Ravens). The relevant rs ranged from approximately .20 through .40. It will be recalled that a categorization consistency composite became available at 4 years of age. This index was also significantly related to WPPSI full scale IQ. MFF error scores also manifested significant inverse relationships with the categorization consistency composite (rs of $-.31$ and $-.51$ for boys and girls, respectively). Given the previously demonstrated linkage between breadth and inconsistency of categorization, it is not surprising to note that MFF error scores were also significantly related to the breadth composite (rs of .38 and .53 for boys and girls, respectively). It is interesting to observe that the MFF latencies exhibited the same pattern as MFF errors in respect to associations with category breadth (negative) and categorization consistency (positive), but the rs were smaller in magnitude. Finally, it should be noted that the field-independence domain has not become completely split off from other Type I styles, for PEFT in girls related significantly to motor inhibition ($r = .27$), whereas RFT scores were significantly associated with MFF error scores in boys ($r = .26$) and with the categorization consistency composite in girls ($r = .26$). However, RFT performance did not relate to either PEFT or IQ scores in the 4-year-olds.

On the whole, the available data on preschoolers clearly point to a substantial overlap between Type I cognitive styles and indices of ability. This is not intended to imply that all of the measures cited can be accommodated by a single dimension or factor. At the present time, however, it is simply not possible to state how many factors are necessary to account for the observed relationships. There clearly appears to be more multidimensionality in the case of the Blocks' findings relative to the results reported in Shipman (1972) for the styles and abilities under consideration. The greater SES heterogeneity in the latter author's sample may have contributed to the foregoing difference.

Messer (1976) tries to account for the modest but consistent relation between MFF errors and EFT scores (although note the exception of the Blocks' 4-year-olds) on the grounds that both contain response uncertainty and require scanning and analysis of a visual field. The attributed similarity, in my view, does not appear credible. Response uncertainty does not seem to be a salient feature of early childhood versions of the EFT (where potentially competing correct choices are minimized), nor is the kind of scanning and visual analysis required in match-to-sample tasks of the MFF variety basically comparable to the processes underlying skill at disembedding (apart from the attentional focusing and persistence demanded in both cases). It would seem more reasonable on the basis of the current state of knowledge to attribute the observed MFF-EFT relationships to uncontrolled age and IQ effects.

B.   TYPE II AND III COGNITIVE STYLES

So far, no attention has been given to Type II styles of conceptualization in relation to other cognitive styles and IQ. In the Kagan *et al.* (1964) monograph empirical evidence is presented in support of a theoretical linkage between preference for an analytic-descriptive style and a disposition toward reflectivity. Although this relationship was subsequently replicated (Ostfeld & Neimark, 1967), its magnitude was quite modest. More recent work by Denney (1972) casts serious doubt on the existence of any relationship whatever between analytic and reflective dispositions. In a sample of second-grade boys, Denney found essentially a zero association between the two styles and these also appeared to function independently when efforts were made to change one or the other style through training. .

Examination of the relationship between descriptive (analytic) and reflective styles for 3- and 4-year-olds in the Block and Block data suggests an equivocal outcome. MFF latency and the descriptive style index from the SOCT were significantly related (r = .39) in the 3-year-old boys. No such relationship emerged for girls at that age, nor were any significant linkages found at 4 years of age. Furthermore, MFF error scores were unrelated to the descriptive index at both 3 and 4 years of age. The overall patterning of these results, in sum, offers only the most limited kind of support to the view that analytic-descriptive conceptualizing and a reflective strategy serve a common cognitive function in early childhood.

Although the indices of breadth and accuracy of categorization derive from the same procedure (Sigel's Object Categorization Test) that is used to assess the three modes of conceptualization, there is no a priori reason to expect relationships to assume a particular form. Data from the Block and Block project, in fact, indicate the absence of any association between breadth (a Type III cognitive style) and the three conceptual styles under study. Accuracy of categorization, however, did relate significantly to the conceptualizing styles. In the case of all four age x sex subsamples, accuracy related significantly to the descriptive (rs ranging from .29 to .62) and to the relational-contextual style (rs ranging from −.33 to −.52). Correlations obtained for the categorical-inferential style were low and negative and attained significance only for the 3-year-olds (rs of −.25 and −.29 for the boys and girls, respectively). It should be noted, finally, that the foregoing relationships between categorization accuracy and conceptual style occurred in the virtual absence of any association between the latter and IQ (the PPVT at age 3 years of age and the WPPSI at 4 years of age).

The foregoing pattern of findings strongly indicates that the descriptive style is an asset and the relational-contextual style is a liability in respect to accuracy of performance on the SOCT, but neither style appears to have much impact in respect to general level of intellective functioning. This raises the possibility, consistent with the Type II status of the conceptual-style domain, of a possible value bias in the scoring procedure. Descriptive groupings by their very nature are close to the physical properties of the stimuli and hence more likely to receive high-accuracy ratings than relational-contextual groupings, which may well assume a more idiosyncratic character. Also of relevance is the consistency of the observed relationships for 3- and 4-year-olds, despite the radical changes in the behavioral correlates of the conceptual styles across the 1-year period. This further reinforces the view that the accuracy-style associations reflect the intrinsic measurement properties of the SOCT rather than genuine psychological linkages between constructs. These are highly speculative inferences, of course, and are offered with a strictly heuristic intent.

In conclusion, it is not possible to go much beyond the truism that the classes of cognitive styles under review are neither completely independent nor completely overlapping in their interrelationships. This is a rather typical outcome, of course, in multivariate studies of individual differences. On the whole, the relationships observed appear to fall into meaningful patterns in the sense that overlap and lack of overlap are congruent to a reasonable degree with the cognitive process tapped by the tasks being related. Intellective ability also enters the picture in conceptually reasonable ways—that is, correlating significantly with Type I but not with Type II and III cognitive styles.

As analysis of the Block and Block data proceeds, we can undoubtedly look forward to further information regarding the multidimensional patterning of cognitive functions in preschoolers. The longitudinal nature of that research, which will extend into the early elementary-school years, will undoubtedly help to clarify the continuities and discontinuities characteristic of that age period. One of the intriguing unknowns at the present time concerns the possibility of deriving a cognitive typology during the early childhood years. It is not unreasonable to expect children to vary in the intraindividual patterning of cognitive dimensions, and this naturally introduces the question of whether a manageable array of stylistic types can be constructed and studied over time during the early childhood years. Block (1971) has profitably taken such an approach in his analysis of the Berkeley growth study data (extending from adolescence into middle adulthood). If it should prove feasible to apply this form of ipsative analysis to the longitudinal data of early childhood, the increment in our understanding of individual variation in children's cognitive functioning may prove to be considerable.[1]

---

[1] In his recent volume on methodology in developmental psychology, Wohlwill (1973) notes with regret the general lack of research of this type and makes a strong plea for the study of "the developmental history of patterns of ipsative relations within a variable set [p. 352]."

VII
Epilogue

The developmental and individual-difference aspects of four cognitive styles, as well as their interrelationships, have received exhaustive treatment in the preceding pages. The conclusions and implications that can be inferred from the research directed toward each style have also been thoroughly discussed. Is there anything further that need be said? Earlier, I indicated that a grand integration of the research on preschoolers' cognitive styles would not be feasible. There is no basis for a radical change in this pessimistic opinion. At the same time, a review of the length represented by the present monograph would surely have to be considered a failure if a few general conclusions or principles could not be extracted from the mass of empirical researches critically summarized in the various chapters of this volume. These conclusions are listed and discussed below.

1. *Sex differences in cognitive styles and strategies are pervasive during the preschool years and almost uniformly favor females.* The relevant data are strongly suggestive of a developmental timetable in which girls are approximately 6 months to 1 year ahead of boys on a variety of cognitive functions. In the few cases where this female superiority does not appear, the alternative is almost always no difference rather than male superiority. It is important to note that the girls' strengths relative to their male age peers is not always manifested in the form of a mean difference. Instead, correlational differences are often critical in the sense of reflecting the emergence of a stable cognitive dimension in girls prior to its appearance in boys.

This conclusion regarding sex differences in early childhood differs somewhat from the view recently offered by Maccoby and Jacklin (1974). Those authors propose that the case for early systematic sex differences in cognitive styles has not been proved. The discrepancy between the Maccoby-Jacklin position and that advanced in this volume is readily explained. Maccoby and Jacklin concentrated almost exclusively on mean sex differences and they apparently did not have access to much of the recent unpublished materials that were available to me. If there are sex differences in the timetable for the emergence of various cognitive dimensions in early childhood, the focus on a mean difference may not be the most appropriate manner to represent the real sex difference at issue. When girls, for example, manifest reasonable stability on some cognitive dimension between the ages of 3 and 4 years, whereas boys show no stability whatever, it is dubious whether mean sex differences obtained at both ages represent comparisons of similar processes.

The demonstration of a pervasive female superiority at the preschool level does not imply that one can explain the basis for it. The notion of a timetable suggests a maturational interpretation. One can also argue, however, that girls relative to boys have simply been better socialized in early childhood for attentiveness and obedience to an adult examiner in a task situation. At the present time, we are better prepared to raise questions than provide answers.

2. *It is inappropriate to treat preschoolers as a homogeneous age group in respect to cognitive styles, for striking changes take place within the preschool period.* This relative lack of stability for a variety of stylistic dimensions seriously complicates the search for infant precursors. Such precursors, assuming that they could be found, would not necessarily be the same for cognitive styles assessed at ages 3 and 5 years. Indeed, one can responsibly question the goal of searching for infant precursors given the knowledge currently in our possession concerning the shifting psychological significance of identically labeled cognitive constructs. The relatively unproductive search for infant precursors of reflection-impulsivity has probably foundered for this very reason.

In the introduction to this monograph (Chapter I), a distinction was drawn between homotypic and heterotypic continuities in developmental research. It was suggested that the search for continuities might have to assume the heterotypic form for ages younger than approximately 27-30 months because linguistic deficits below that age would make it impossible to administer the conventional stylistic assessors. A correction is now clearly in order. Studies have indicated that categorization can be found in children between 12 and 24 months of age, well before the child can genuinely understand experimental instructions and apply verbal labels to his categorizations. Several investigators have in fact demonstrated that categorization tasks can be administered to infants as young as 1-4 months of age.

The demonstration of the foregoing skills in very young children (that is, what appear to be homotypic continuities for breadth of categorization and styles of conceptualization) in no sense implies a common process bridging this and analogous performances of older children. Just as an infant's cry may have a distinctly different meaning at 1 month and 1 year of age, so may there be widely varying significance to breadth of categorization at 18 months and 3 years of age. The truth of the matter, of course, is that we simply do not know. The longitudinal research essential to answer the question has not yet been carried out.

3. *The links between cognitive styles, on the one hand, and personality and socioemotional behaviors, on the other, are abundant and multifaceted, but these relationships do not necessarily remain constant either within the preschool period or across preschool and later ages.* It should be further noted that cognition-personality relationships do not assume the same form in preschool boys and girls. The task for the future is to try to account for this differential sex patterning. On the whole, the model proposed several years ago by Maccoby (1966) to account for sex differences in cognition-personality relationships has not fared well. The data reviewed in this volume run counter to it, and Maccoby and Jacklin (1974) seem to have forsaken it in their current compendium. Those authors still cling to the view, however, that assertiveness and a sense of internal control are more likely to contribute to superior cognitive performance in girls than in boys. That general proposition does receive some support in the preceding chapters but far from unequivocal support.

It is the striking age effects in the patterning of cognition-personality relationships that testify to the changing psychological meaning attaching to cognitive styles and strategies over the course of development. The reasons for such change remain elusive, however. Why should an analytic-descriptive style of conceptualization be associated with a set of highly positive socioemotional behaviors at one period during the preschool years only to lose or reverse such associations 1 year later? Here is where the one cognitive variable at a time strategy fails to do justice to the complexity of the problem. If we could derive a limited number of syndromes or types of cognitive patterning at one age (let us say 3 years, for example), longitudinal followup a year or more later might prove highly informative in respect to the basis for stability and change.

4. *Although IQ by virtue of modest links to the cognitive-style domain does have an impact on cognition-personality relationships, its role seems to be a limited one.* There is little doubt that a global IQ construct can account for only a small portion of the variance in the cognitive performance of preschoolers. It is not surprising that IQ relates to Type I cognitive styles in preschoolers, for such relationships are also observed in adults. Where partial correlation techniques are applied, however, it does not appear that linkages between cognitive styles and social behavior disappear. Although such techniques are to be recommended for separating stylistic and ability variance, we should not lose sight of the fact that the issue of causal direction has not been settled. Stylistic or strategic dispositions may contribute to performance on IQ tests, instead of IQ level exerting an influence on cognitive styles. New techniques have been developed for assessing the causal direction of relationships in correlational

data of a longitudinal character. For example, cross-lagged panel analysis (e.g., Rozelle & Campbell, 1969) could easily be applied to much of the longitudinal data reviewed earlier. Although such techniques are not without flaws, the demonstration of one-way directional effects across diverse samples and variables can help to clarify the ability-style interaction. The data are currently at hand for the kinds of tests described.

The evidence in respect to mental age (cognitive developmental level) is considerably more equivocal. The one study that obtained strong MA effects (Achenbach & Weisz, 1975) used a sample with a broad age range and did not control for chronological age. There is an obvious need for further research on the influence of the MA variable in a context where the role of CA can also be examined. Note, finally, that the issue of causal directionality is as unsettled for MA as it is for IQ.

5. *The notion that the stylistic preferences of later childhood turn into capacities in early childhood appears to be exaggerated.* Where Type II and Type III cognitive styles are concerned, the evidence for ease of modifiability of cognitive functioning can be found in children as young as 2 years of age. That the provision of brief training (such as modeling of the desired performance by the examiner) can result in radical changes in style indicates the degree to which performance may not be reflective of potential competence. If certain styles do not exist within the repertoire of the young child, it often does not take much effort to install them there. Furthermore, we may sometimes find that the child can find an alternative method for performing a task by simply asking him or her to do so. It makes no sense to assess the stylistic preferences of children and to treat them as comparable to capacities when no effort has been made to exhaust the repertoire of the child. We have seen how the developmental curves for styles of conceptualization change when subjects are asked to group in all possible ways instead of strictly in the most preferred way.

One is entitled to inquire at this juncture whether the combination of optimal methods of assessment and exhaustion of the child's repertoire would drastically curtail the extent of individual differences in particular cognitive-style domains. Unfortunately, it is not possible to answer this question without carrying out the relevant study. We may find that subject rank orders do not change, although a constant has been added to everyone's performance. Alternatively, rank orders of subjects may be disrupted, the new ordering now indicative of a capacity rather than a stylistic preference.

6. *The current developmental evidence in respect to categorization and conceptualization does not support the proposition of unilinear sequences; a multilinear model of development appears to be more appropriate.* Until quite recently, it has been assumed that breadth of categorization must proceed in one direction—development brings greater breadth or lesser breadth (depending on one's theoretical perspective). In a similar fashion, many developmentalists have presumed that the younger child uses perceptual attributes in

classifying, whereas the older child shifts to functional attributes. As investigators have extended their research to children younger than 3 years, it has become strikingly clear that dispositions typical of older children can be found in rudimentary form in children considerably younger in age.

Early styles do not drop out of the child's repertoire but continuously reemerge in more complex and sophisticated forms over the life span. This is the basic idea of multilinear development originally advanced by Heinz Werner (1957) a number of years ago, and is at the core of Riegel's (1973) dialectical theory of cognitive development.

7. *The measurement of cognitive styles in early childhood is strongly influenced by variations in task content and stimulus materials.* Unlike school-age children who have become quite accustomed to working on cognitive tasks, the preschool child in an experimental test-taking context is likely to be facing a quite novel situation. Demand characteristics of the task and the context assume considerable importance under these circumstances, and we can expect that the child's performance may sometimes be telling us more about these external influences than about cognitive structures as such. This is not to imply that all tasks are likely to have a decidedly alien quality for young children; one can, of course, employ materials similar to those the child uses in play. Nevertheless, the striking differences that are sometimes manifested between data obtained from naturalistic and experimental sources represents a tribute to the young child's sensitivity or susceptibility to environmental contingencies. Other indications of the importance of task content derive from studies showing variation in performance as a function of changes in format of administration (for example, removing the head constraints in the portable rod-and-frame apparatus), in experimental instructions (for example, forming all possible groupings rather than just the preferred grouping), in clarification of task requirements (for example, the experimenter illustrating task solution on a sample problem), and in nature of stimulus materials (for example, words versus pictures).

Should one conclude from the foregoing examples that a strictly situational approach to cognitive performance is adequate to handle the present domain? This would be a truly astonishing conclusion, particularly when it is recalled that Mischel (1968) specifically has excluded the cognitive domain from the operation of social learning principles. An interactionist approach (e.g., Bowers, 1973) appears to be a more reasonable alternative, although it must be recognized that the typical methodology employed (the extraction of person, situation, and person x situation variance components) has so far ignored developmental level as a source of variance.

It should be noted that the moderator variable approach (e.g., Kogan & Wallach, 1964) has not yet been applied at the level of early childhood, except for such demographic variables as sex, socioeconomic status, and ethnic or cultural group. Yet, it is not at all out of the question that the limited coherence among diverse indicators of cognitive-style constructs in early childhood disguises separate subgroups of children, some of whom exhibit considerable coherence, the remainder of the sample showing no coherence whatever. Theoretical ingenuity will be required, of course, to tease out the kinds of variables likely to function in a moderator role. The variables that have functioned in this manner in adulthood (for example, test anxiety and defensiveness) may not necessarily work in early childhood. Task and context parameters can also serve as moderators, of course, and it is quite feasible that coherence among indicators of particular cognitive styles can be more easily facilitated along such lines than by searching for relevant intrapsychic moderators. Research on moderator effects is likely to be a high-risk enterprise, but its success may represent an enormous increase in our understanding of the basis for individual differences in young children's cognitive styles.

The time has clearly come to draw this volume to a close. Despite its aim of exhaustive coverage, certain topics have failed to receive the extended treatment that they deserve. Occasional reference has been made to social class, for example, but a thorough analysis of the impact of that important demographic variable on cognitive styles has not been attempted. Similarly, cross-cultural evidence has been given little emphasis. This is a serious shortcoming, to be sure, for research in less developed societies offers unparalleled opportunities for validating cognitive-style indices against natural ecological indicators. For example, there is evidence that children of the Logoli and Gusii tribes of Kenya (varying in age from 3 to 8 years) who perform at a higher level on copying block patterns and geometric forms (tasks likely to be strongly related to field independence) tend to wander greater distances from home during their free time (Munroe & Munroe, 1971; Nerlove, Munroe & Munroe, 1971). More recently, a study of rural Guatemalan children 5-8 years of age (Nerlove, Roberts, Klein, Yarbrough, & Habicht, 1974) demonstrated significant relationships between analytic ability[1] and self-managed behavioral sequences in work and play (as rated by trained observers).

Although all of the foregoing studies hold great theoretical promise, they tend to suffer from a lack of adequate control over the chronological.age variable. Even when the cognitive measures are controlled for the age dimension (as in Nerlove et al., 1974), the strong possibility remains that such variables as distance traveled from home and initiation of self-managed sequences are more characteristic of 7- than of 5-year-olds, for example. Apart from these methodological considerations, however, it is difficult to articulate the foregoing research with data on children from urbanized Western societies. This volume has focused on preschoolers, that is, children 5 years of age and younger. Given

[1]This consisted of a combined index of the CEFT score (number correct) and the MFF error score. Although the consistent significant association observed between those variables (see Chapter VI) justifies their empirical combination, the application of the label "analytic ability" can be questioned. It is regrettable that separate correlations for CEFT and MFF were not reported.

the erratic patterns of schooling in less developed cultures, however, the preschool period cannot be designated in chronological-age terms. This is a considerable advantage, of course, when the focus is on the effects of schooling (e.g., Bruner et al., 1966) but is a major complication from the perspective of this volume. The reader interested in the impact of cross-cultural differences would be well advised to consult the Cole and Scribner (1974) volume for cognition broadly conceived and the Witkin and Berry (1975) paper for field independence-dependence specifically.

A final lack—perhaps the most serious of all—is the general neglect of the cohort problem. The preschooler in America today is unquestionably subject to a set of sociocultural forces (transmitted through the family, the nursery school, and the mass media) differing in important respects from those impinging on the preschooler of a generation ago. Sophisticated designs are now available for disentangling the impact of cohort membership and ontogenetic change on cognitive performance (e.g., Baltes, 1968; Baltes & Reinert, 1969). Such studies have so far been confined to older children and adults. Yet, there is no reason why the cohort versus ontogenetic distinction should be less important for preschoolers than for older subjects. Who would dare to claim, for example, that "Sesame Street" has had absolutely no effect on recent cohorts of preschoolers?

Attention must also be paid to Wohlwill's (1973) claim that research on individual differences in childhood has told us more about stability and change in psychological dimensions than about the actual developmental course of individual children. The frequent citation of correlation coefficients throughout this volume is obviously in support of Wohlwill's assertion. It cannot be denied that we know much more about the stability of cognitive styles over time in the sense of extent of constancy in the interindividual rank ordering of children than we know about possible similarities or differences among children in rates and patterns of change on cognitive-style dimensions. Yet it would be most surprising if children did not vary in the latter respect, and it would obviously be of considerable interest to explore the correlates and determinants of such change. Individual-difference researchers who undertake longitudinal studies have typically been preoccupied with the continuity of their favorite variables over time to the virtual exclusion of a more child-centered developmental function approach. Wohlwill's methodological recommendations, if heeded, would help to restore a more balanced perspective.

Although this volume has depended heavily on recent unpublished materials, its rate of obsolescence is sure to be rapid. Research on cognitive styles and associated dimensions in preschoolers continues unabated. It will not be long before longitudinal data become available that bridge the preschool and early school-age periods. The field is almost certain to require another full-scale review in the not too distant future, and a more definitive integration should be possible at that time. I would delight in the eventual appearance of such a review and would be one of its most avid readers.

References

Achenbach, T. M., & Weisz, J. R. Impulsivity-reflectivity and cognitive development in preschoolers: A longitudinal analysis of developmental and trait variance. *Developmental Psychology,* 1975, *11,* 413-414.

Annett, M. The classification of instances of four common class concepts by children and adults. *British Journal of Educational Psychology,* 1959, *29,* 223-236.

Ault, R. L., Crawford, D. E., & Jeffrey, W. E. Visual scanning strategies of reflective, impulsive, fast-accurate and slow-inaccurate children on the Matching Familiar Figures test. *Child Development,* 1972, *43,* 1412-1417.

Ault, R. L., Mitchell, C., & Hartmann, D. P. Some methodological problems in reflection-impulsivity research. *Child Development,* 1976, *47,* 227-231.

Baird, R. R., & Bee, H. L. Modification of conceptual styles preference by differential reinforcement. *Child Development,* 1969, *40,* 903-910.

Ball, S., & Bogatz, G. A. Summative research of *Sesame Street:* Implications for the study of preschool children. In A. D. Pick (Ed.), *Minnesota symposia on child psychology.* Vol. 6. Minneapolis: University of Minnesota Press, 1972.

Baltes, P. B. Longitudinal and cross-sectional sequences in the study of age and generation effects. *Human Development,* 1968, *11,* 145-171.

Baltes, P. B., & Reinert, G. Cohort effects in cognitive development of children as revealed by cross-sectional sequences. *Developmental Psychology,* 1969, *1,* 169-177.

Banta, T. J. Tests for the evaluation of early childhood education: The Cincinnati Autonomy Test Battery (CATB). In J. Hellmuth (Ed.), *Cognitive studies.* Vol. 1. New York: Brunner-Mazel, 1970.

Bayley, N. Development of mental abilities. In P. Mussen (Ed.), *Carmichael's manual of child psychology.* Vol. 1. New York: Wiley, 1970.

Bell, R. Q. A reinterpretation of the direction of the effects in studies of socialization. *Psychological Review,* 1968, *75,* 81-95.

Bell, R. Q., Weller, G. M., & Waldrop, M. F. Newborn and preschoolers: Organization of behavior and relations between periods. *Monographs of the Society for Research in Child Development,* 1971, *36*(1-2, Serial No. 142).

Berlyne, D. E. *Conflict, arousal, and curiosity.* New York: McGraw-Hill, 1960.

Bernstein, B. Social class and linguistic development: A theory of social learning. In A. H. Halsey, J. Floud, & C. A. Anderson (Eds.), *Education, economy and society.* Glencoe, Illinois: Free Press, 1961.

Bieri, J. Complexity-simplicity as a personality variable in cognitive and preferential behavior. In D. W. Fiske & S. R. Maddi (Eds.), *Functions of varied experience.* Homewood, Illinois: Dorsey, 1961.

Bieri, J. Cognitive complexity and personality development. In O. J. Harvey (Ed.), *Experience, structure and adaptability.* New York: Springer, 1966.

Bieri, J. Category width as a measure of discrimination. *Journal of Personality,* 1969, *37*, 513-521.

Bieri, J. Cognitive structures in personality. In H. M. Schroder & P. Suedfeld (Eds.), *Personality theory and information processing.* New York: Ronald Press, 1971.

Blank, M. Eliciting verbalization from young children in experimental tasks: A methodological note. *Child Development,* 1975, *46*, 254-257.

Block, J. *The Q-sort method in personality assessment and psychiatric research.* Springfield, Illinois: Charles C Thomas, 1961.

Block, J. *The challenge of response sets.* New York: Appleton-Century-Crofts, 1965.

Block, J. *Lives through time.* Berkeley: Bancroft Books, 1971.

Block, J., & Block, J. H. Ego development and the provenance of thought. NIMH Progress Report (Grant No. M. H. 16080), University of California, Berkeley, 1973.

Block, J., Block, J. H., & Harrington, D. M. Some misgivings about the Matching Familiar Figures test as a measure of reflection-impulsivity. *Developmental Psychology,* 1974, *10*, 611-632.

Block, J., Block, J. H., & Harrington, D. M. Comment on the Kagan-Messer reply. *Developmental Psychology,* 1975, *11*, 249-252.

Block, J., & Petersen, P. Some personality correlates of confidence, caution, and speed in a decision situation. *Journal of Abnormal and Social Psychology,* 1955, *51*, 34-41.

Bornstein, M. H. Qualities of color vision in infancy. *Journal of Experimental Child Psychology,* 1975, *19*, 401-419.

Bornstein, M. H., Kessen, W., & Weiskopf, S. A. The categories of hue in infancy. *Science,* 1976, *191*, 201-202.

Bowers, K. S. Situationism in psychology: An analysis and a critique. *Psychological Review,* 1973, *80*, 307-336.

Britain, S. D., Dunkel, J., & Coull, B. Perceptual training of field-dependent and field-independent 5-year-olds: An increase in analytic visual ability. Paper presented at the Biennial Meeting of the Society for Research in Child Development, Denver, April 1975.

Bruner, J. S., Olver, R. R., & Greenfield, P. M. *Studies in cognitive growth.* New York: Wiley, 1966.

Buffery, A. W. H., & Gray, J. A. Gender differences in the development of spatial and linguistic skills. In C. Ounsted & D. C. Taylor (Eds.), *Gender differences: Their ontogeny and significance.* London: Churchill, 1972.

Cattell, R. *The IPAT Test of "g": Culture-free, scale 1.* Champaign-Urbana, Illinois: University of Illinois, Institute for Personality and Ability Testing, 1950.

Cicirelli, V. G. Effect of sibling structure and interaction on children's categorization style. *Developmental Psychology,* 1973, *9*, 132-139.

Clark, E. V. What's in a word? On the child's acquisition of semantics in his first language. In T. E. Moore (Ed.), *Cognitive development and the acquisition of language.* New York: Academic Press, 1973.

Coates, S. *Preschool Embedded Figures Test.* Palo Alto, California: Consulting Psychologists Press, 1972.

Coates, S. Sex differences in field independence among preschool children. In R. C. Fried-
man, R. M. Richart, & R. L. Vande Wiele (Eds.), *Sex differences in behavior.* New York:
Wiley, 1974.   (a)

Coates, S. Sex differences in field dependence-independence between the ages of 3 and 6.
Perceptual and Motor Skills, 1974, *39,* 1307-1310.   (b)

Coates, S. Field independence and intellectual functioning in preschool children. *Perceptual
and Motor Skills,* 1975, *41,* 251-254.

Coates, S., & Bromberg, P. M. The factorial structure of the WPPSI between the ages of 4
and 6½. *Journal of Consulting and Clinical Psychology,* 1973, *40,* 365-370.

Coates, S., & Lord, M. Field-independence, autonomy striving, aggression, and sex differences in preschool children. Unpublished manuscript, State University of New York,
Downstate Medical Center, 1973.

Coates, S., Lord, M., & Jakabovics, E. Field dependence-independence, social-nonsocial
play, and sex differences in preschool children. *Perceptual and Motor Skills,* 1975,
40, 195-202.

Cole, M., & Scribner, S. *Culture and thought: A psychological introduction.* New York:
Wiley, 1974.

Cooperative Tests and Services. *Preschool Inventory revised edition-1970: Handbook.*
Princeton, New Jersey: Educational Testing Service, 1970.

Corah, N. L. Differentiation in children and their parents. *Journal of Personality,* 1965,
33, 300-308.

Crandall, J. E. Some relationships among sex, anxiety and conservatism of judgement.
Journal of Personality, 1965, *33,* 99-107.

Crandall, V. J., & Sinkeldam, C. Children's dependent and achievement behaviors in social
situations and their perceptual field dependence. *Journal of Personality,* 1964, *32,*
1-22.

Davidson, K. S., & Sarason, S. B. Text anxiety and classroom observations. *Child Development,* 1961, *32,* 199-210.

Davis, A. J. Cognitive styles: Methodological and developmental considerations. *Child
Development,* 1971, *42,* 1447-1459.

Davis, A. J., & Lange, G. Parent-child communication and the development of categorization styles in preschool children. *Child Development,* 1973, *44,* 624-629.

Denney, D. R. The assessment of differences in conceptual style. *Child Study Journal,*
1971, *1,* 142-155.

Denney, D. R. Modeling effects upon conceptual style and cognitive tempo. *Child Development,* 1972, *43,* 105-119.

Denney, N. W. A developmental study of free classification in children. *Child Development,*
1972, *43,* 221-232.   (a)

Denney, N. W. Free classification in preschool children. *Child Development,* 1972, *43,*
1161-1170.   (b)

Denney, N. W. Evidence for developmental changes in categorization criteria for children
and adults. *Human Development,* 1974, *17,* 41-53.

Denney, N. W., & Acito, M. A. Classification training in two- and three-year-old children.
Journal of Experimental Child Psychology, 1974, *17,* 37-48.

Dermen, D., & Meissner, J. A. Preschool Embedded Figures Test. In V. C. Shipman (Ed.),
Disadvantaged children and their first school experiences. (PR-72-27.) Princeton, New
Jersey: Educational Testing Service, 1972.

Donaldson, M., & Wales, R. J. On the acquisition of some relational terms. In J. R. Hayes
(Ed.), *Cognition and the development of language.* New York: Wiley, 1970.

Drake, D. M. Perceptual correlates of impulsive and reflective behavior. *Developmental
Psychology,* 1970, *2,* 202-214.

Dreyer, A. S. Family interaction and cognitive style: Situation and cross-sex effects. Paper presented at the Biennial Meeting of the Society for Research in Child Development, Denver, April 1975.

Dreyer, A. S., Dreyer, C. A., & Nebelkopf, E. B. Portable rod-and-frame test as a measure of cognitive style in kindergarten children. *Perceptual and Motor Skills*, 1971, *33*, 775-781.

Dreyer, A. S., McIntire, W. G., & Dreyer, C. A. Sociometric status and cogitive. style in kindergarten children. *Perceptual and Motor Skills*, 1973, *37*, 407-412.

Dunn, L. M. *Expanded manual, Peabody Picture Vocabulary Test.* Circle Pines, Minn.: American Guidance Service, 1965.

Eimas, P. D., Siqueland, E. R., Jusczyk, P., & Vigorito, J. Speech perception in infants. *Science*, 1971, *171*, 303-306.

Emmerich, W. Continuity and stability in early social development. *Child Development*, 1964, *35*, 311-332.

Emmerich, W. Personality development and concepts of structure. *Child Development*, 1968, *39*, 671-690.

Escalona, S. K. *The roots of individuality: Normal patterns of development in infancy.* Chicago: Aldine, 1968.

Eska, B., & Black, K. N. Conceptual tempo in young grade-school children. *Child Development*, 1971, *42*, 505-516.

Farnham-Diggory, S., & Gregg, L. W. Color, form, and function as dimensions of natural classification: Developmental changes in eye movements, reaction time, and response strategies. *Child Development*, 1975, *46*, 101-114.

Faterson, H. F., & Witkin, H. A. Longitudinal study of development of the body concept. *Developmental Psychology*, 1970, *2*, 429-438.

Fillenbaum, S. Some stylistic aspects of categorizing behavior. *Journal of Personality*, 1959, *27*, 187-195.

Fiske, D. W., & Maddi, S. R. (Eds.) *Functions of varied experience.* Homewood, Illinois: Dorsey, 1961.

Flavell, J. H., Botkin, P. T., Fry, C. L., Wright, J. W., & Jarvis, P. E. *The development of role-taking and communication skills in children.* New York: Wiley, 1968.

Ford, M. A., Stern, D. N., & Dillon, D. J. Performance of children ages 3 to 5 on the Draw-a-Person task: Sex differences. *Perceptual and Motor Skills*, 1974, *38*, 1188.

Fuqua, R. W., Bartsch, T. W., & Phye, G. D. An investigation of the relationship between cognitive tempo and creativity in preschool-age children. *Child Development*, 1975, *46*, 779-782.

Gardner, R. W. Cognitive styles in categorizing behavior. *Journal of Personality*, 1953, *22*, 214-233.

Gardner, R. W., Holzman, P. S., Klein, G. S., Linton, H. B., & Spence, D. P. Cognitive control: A study of individual consistencies in cognitive behavior. *Psychological Issues*, 1959, *1* (Monograph 4).

Gardner, R. W., & Moriarty, A. E. *Personality development at preadolescence.* Seattle: University of Washington Press, 1968.

Gardner, R. W., & Schoen, R. A. Differentiation and abstraction in concept formation. *Psychological Monographs*, 1962, *76*(41, Whole No. 560).

Garrett, H. E. A developmental theory of intelligence. *American Psychologist*, 1946, *1*, 372-378.

Gibson, E. J. *Principles of perceptual learning and development.* New York: Appleton-Century-Crofts, 1969.

Gibson, J. J., & Gibson, E. J. Perceptual learning: Differentiation or enrichment? *Psychological Review*, 1955, *62*, 32-41. ·

Gilbert, L. E., & Shipman, V. C. Preschool Inventory. In V. C. Shipman (Ed.), *Disadvantaged children and their first school experiences.* (PR-72-27.) Princeton, New Jersey: Educational Testing Service, 1972.

Glixman, A. F. Categorizing behavior as a function of meaning domain. *Journal of Personality and Social Psychology*, 1965, *2*, 370-377.

Goldman, A. E., & Levine, M. A developmental study of object sorting. *Child Development*, 1963, *34*, 649-666.

Goodenough, D. R., & Karp, S. A. Field dependence and intellectual functioning. *Journal of Abnormal and Social Psychology*, 1961, *63*, 241-246.

Guilford, J. P. *The nature of human intelligence.* New York: McGraw-Hill, 1967.

Harrison, A., & Nadelman, L. Conceptual tempo and inhibition of movement in black preschool children. *Child Development*, 1972, *43*, 657-668.

Hartmann, H. *Ego psychology and the problem of adaptation.* New York: International Universities Press, 1958.

Harvey, O. J., Hunt, D. E., & Schroder, H. M. *Conceptual systems and personality organization.* New York: Wiley, 1961.

Haskins, R., & McKinney, J. D. Relative effects of response tempo and accuracy on problem solving and academic achievement. *Child Development*, 1976, *47*, in press.

Heider, E. R. "Focal" color areas and the development of color names. *Developmental Psychology*, 1971, *4*, 447-455.

Heider, E. R. Universals in color naming and memory. *Journal of Experimental Psychology*, 1972, *93*, 10-20.

Heise, D. R. Problems in path analysis and causal inference. In E. F. Borgatta & G. W. Bohrnstedt (Eds.), *Sociological methodology*, San Francisco: Jossey-Bass, 1969.

Hess, R. D., & Shipman, V. C. Early experience and the socialization of cognitive modes in children. *Child Development*, 1965, *36*, 869-886.

Hess, R. D., & Shipman, V. C. Cognitive elements in maternal behavior. In J. P. Hill (Ed.), *Minnesota symposia on child psychology.* Vol. 1. Minneapolis: University of Minnesota Press, 1967.

Hunt, J. McV. Intrinsic motivation and its role in psychological development. In D. Levine (Ed.), *Nebraska Symposium on Motivation.* Vol. 13. Lincoln: University of Nebraska Press, 1965.

Inhelder, B., & Piaget, J. *The early growth of logic in the child.* New York: Harper and Row, 1964.

Jennings, K. D. People versus object orientation, social behavior, and intellectual abilities in preschool children. *Developmental Psychology*, 1975, *11*, 511-519.

Kagan, J. Individual differences in the resolution of response uncertainty. *Journal of Personality and Social Psychology*, 1965, *2*, 154-160.

Kagan, J. Developmental studies of reflection and analysis. In A. H. Kidd & J. L. Rivoire (Eds.), *Perceptual development in children.* New York: International Universities Press, 1966.

Kagan, J. Biological aspects of inhibition systems. *American Journal of Diseases of Children*, 1967, *114*, 507-512.

Kagan, J. *Change and continuity in infancy.* New York: Wiley, 1971.

Kagan, J., & Kogan, N. Individual variation in cognitive processes. In P. Mussen (Ed.), *Carmichael's manual of child psychology.* Vol. 1. New York: Wiley, 1970.

Kagan, J., & Messer, S. B. A reply to "Some misgivings about the Matching Familiar Figures test as a measure of reflection-impulsivity." *Developmental Psychology*, 1975, *11*, 244-248.

Kagan, J., Moss, H. A., & Sigel, I. E. Psychological significance of styles of conceptualization. In J. C. Wright & J. Kagan (eds.), Basic cognitive processes in children. *Monographs of the Society for Research in Child Development*, 1963, *28* (2, Serial No. 86), 73-112.

graphs of the Society for Research in Child Development, 1963, *28* (2, Serial No. 86), 73-112.

Kagan, J., Rosman, B. L., Day, D., Albert, J., & Phillips, W. Information processing in the child: Significance of analytic and reflective attitudes. *Psychological Monographs*, 1964, *78*(1, Whole No. 578).

Karp, S. A., & Konstadt, N. L. *Manual for the Children's Embedded Figures Test.* Brooklyn, New York: Cognitive Tests, 1963.

Katz, J. M. Reflection-impulsivity and color-form sorting. *Child Development*, 1971, *42*, 745-754.

Katz, J. M. Cognitive tempo and discrimination skill on color-form sorting tasks. *Perceptual and Motor Skills*, 1972, *35*, 359-362.

Kennedy, K., & Kates, S. L. Conceptual sorting and personality adjustment in children. *Journal of Abnormal and Social Psychology*, 1964, *68*, 211-214.

Kerlinger, F. N., & Pedhazur, E. J. *Multiple regression in behavioral research.* New York: Holt, Rinehart & Winston, 1973.

Klein, G. S. *Perception, motives, and personality.* New York: Knopf, 1970.

Klein, G. S., & Schlesinger, H. J. Perceptual attitudes toward instability. I: Prediction of apparent movement experiences from Rorschach responses. *Journal of Personality*, 1951, *19*, 289-302.

Kogan, N. Educational implications of cognitive styles. In G. S. Lesser (Ed.), *Psychology and educational practice.* Glenview, Illinois: Scott, Foresman, 1971.

Kogan, N. Creativity and cognitive style: A life span perspective. In P. Baltes & K. W. Schaie (Eds.), *Life span developmental psychology: Personality and socialization.* New York: Academic Press, 1973.

Kogan, N. Sex differences in creativity and cognitive styles. In S. Messick (Ed.), *Individuality in learning: Cognitive styles and creativity for human development.* San Francisco: Jossey-Bass, 1976.

Kogan, N., & Wallach, M. A. *Risk taking: A study in cognition and personality.* New York: Holt, Rinehart & Winston, 1964.

Konstadt, N., & Forman, E. Field dependence and external directedness. *Journal of Personality and Social Psychology*, 1965, *1*, 490-493.

Korner, A. F. Some hypotheses regarding the significance of individual differences at birth for later development. In *Psychoanalytic study of the child.* Vol. 19. New York: International Universities Press, 1964.

Lenneberg, E. H. *Biological foundations of language.* New York: Wiley, 1967.

Levine, M. Hypothesis behavior in humans during discrimination learning. *Journal of Experimental Psychology*, 1966, *71*, 331-338.

Lewis, M. The meaning of a response, or why researchers in infant behavior should be Oriental metaphysicians. *Merrill-Palmer Quarterly*, 1967, *13*, 7-18.

Lewis, M., Rausch, M., Goldberg, S., & Dodd, C. Error, response time, and IQ: Sex differences in the cognitive style of preschool children. *Perceptual and Motor Skills*, 1968, *26*, 563-568.

Lewis, M., & Rosenblum, L. A. (Eds.) *The effects of the infant on its caregiver.* New York: Wiley, 1974.

Lindstrom, D. R., & Shipman, V. C. Sigel Object Categorization Test. In V. C. Shipman (Ed.), *Disadvantaged children and their first school experiences.* (PR-72-27.) Princeton, New Jersey: Educational Testing Service, 1972.

Maccoby, E. E. Sex differences in intellectual functioning. In E. E. Maccoby (Ed.), *The development of sex differences.* Stanford, California: Stanford University Press, 1966.

Maccoby, E. E., Dowley, E. M., Hagen, J. W., & Degerman, R. Activity level and intellectual functioning in normal preschool children. *Child Development*, 1965, *36*, 761-770.

Maccoby, E. E., & Jacklin, C. N. *The psychology of sex differences.* Stanford, Calif.: Stanford University Press, 1974.

Mann, L. Differences between reflective and impulsive children in tempo and quality of decision making. *Child Development*, 1973, *44*, 274-279.

Massari, D., Hayweiser, L., & Meyer, W. Activity level and intellectual functioning in deprived preschool children. *Developmental Psychology*, 1969, *1*, 286-290.

Massari, D., & Massari, J. A. Sex differences in the relationship of cognitive style and intellectual functioning in disadvantaged preschool children. *Journal of Genetic Psychology*, 1973, *122*, 175-181.

McCall, R. B., Hogarty, P. S., & Hurlburt, N. Transitions in infant sensorimotor development and the prediction of childhood IQ. *American Psychologist*, 1972, *27*, 728-748.

McCluskey, K. A., & Wright, J. C. Age and reflection-impulsivity as determinants of selective and relevant observing behavior. Paper presented at the Biennial Meeting of the Society for Research in Child Development, Philadelphia, March 1973.

McReynolds, P. The concept evaluation technique: A survey of research. *Journal of General Psychology*, 1966, *74*, 217-230.

Meichenbaum, D. H., & Goodman, J. Reflection-impulsivity and verbal control of motor behavior. *Child Development*, 1969, *40*, 785-797.

Mervis, C. B., Catlin, J., and Rosch, E. Development of the structure of color categories. *Developmental Psychology*, 1975, *11*, 54-60.

Messer, S. The effect of anxiety over intellectual performance on reflection-impulsivity in children. *Child Development*, 1970, *41*, 723-735.

Messer, S. Reflection-impulsivity: A review. *Psychological Bulletin*, 1976, *83*, in press.

Messick, S. The criterion problem in the evaluation of instruction: Assessing possible, not just intended, outcomes. In M. C. Wittrock & D. Wiley (Eds.), *The evaluation of instruction: Issues and problems.* New York: Holt, Rinehart & Winston, 1970.

Messick, S. Multivariate models of cognition and personality: The need for both process and structure in psychological theory and measurement. In J. R. Royce (Ed.), *Multivariate analysis and psychological theory.* New York: Academic Press, 1973.

Messick, S., & Damarin, F. Cognitive styles and memory for faces. *Journal of Abnormal and Social Psychology*, 1964, *69*, 313-318.

Messick, S., & Kogan, N. Differentiation and compartmentalization in object sorting measures of categorizing styles. *Perceptual and Motor Skills*, 1963, *16*, 47-51.

Messick, S., & Kogan, N. Category width and quantitative aptitude. *Perceptual and Motor Skills*, 1965, *20*, 493-497.

Meyers, C. E., Dingman, H. F., Orpet, R. E., Sitkei, E., & Watts, C. A. Four ability-factor hypotheses at three preliterate levels in normal and retarded children. *Monographs of the Society for Research in Child Development*, 1964, *29*(5, Serial No. 96).

Mischel, W. *Personality and assessment.* New York: Wiley, 1968.

Mumbauer, C. C., & Miller, J. O. Socioeconomic background and cognitive functioning in preschool children. *Child Development*, 1970, *41*, 471-480.

Munroe, R. H., & Munroe, R. L. Effect of environmental experience on spatial ability in an East African society. *Journal of Social Psychology*, 1971, *83*, 15-22.

Munroe, R. H., & Munroe, R. L. Infant care and childhood performance in East Africa. Paper presented at the Biennial Meeting of the Society for Research in Child Development, Denver, April 1975.

Murphy, L. B. *The widening world of childhood: Paths toward mastery.* New York: Basic Books, 1962.

Neimark, E. D. Natural language concepts: Additional evidence. *Child Development*, 1974, *45*, 508-511.

Nelson, K. Structure and strategy in learning to talk. *Monographs of the Society for Research in Child Development*, 1973, *38*(1-2, Serial No. 149). (a)

Nelson, K. Some evidence for the cognitive primacy of categorization and its functional basis. *Merrill-Palmer Quarterly*, 1973, *19*, 21-39.   (b)

Nelson, K. Variations in children's concepts by age and category. *Child Development*, 1974, *45*, 577-584.   (a)

Nelson, K. Concept, word, and sentence: Interrelations in acquisition and development. *Psychological Review*, 1974, *81*, 267-285.   (b)

Nelson, K. E., & Bonvillian, J. D. Concepts and words in the 18-month-old: Acquiring concept names under controlled conditions. *Cognition*, 1973, *2*, 435-450.

Nerlove, S. B., Munroe, R. H., & Munroe, R. L. Effect of environmental experience on spatial ability: A replication. *Journal of Social Psychology*, 1971, *84*, 3-10.

Nerlove, S. B., Roberts, J. M., Klein, R. E., Yarbrough, C., & Habicht, J. Natural indicators of cognitive development: An observational study of rural Guatemalan children. *Ethos*, 1974, *2*, 265-295.

Nunnally, J. C., & Lemond, L. C. Exploratory behavior and human development. In L. P. Lipsitt & H. W. Reese (Eds.), *Advances in child development and behavior*. Vol. 8. New York: Academic Press, 1973.

Odom, R. D., McIntyre, C. W., & Neale, G. S. The influence of cognitive style on perceptual learning, *Child Development*, 1971, *42*, 883-891.

Oltman, P. K. A portable rod-and-frame apparatus. *Perceptual and Motor Skills*, 1968, *26*, 503-506.

Ostfeld, B. M., & Neimark, E. D. Effect of response time restriction upon cognitive style scores. *Proceedings of the 75th Annual Convention of the American Psychological Association*, 1967, *2*, 169-170.

Palmer, F., & Rees, A. Concept training in two-year-olds: Procedure and results. Paper presented at the Biennial Meeting of the Society for Research in Child Development, Santa Monica, California, March 1969.

Paul, E. A study of the relationship between separation and field dependency in a group of three-year-old nursery-school children. Unpublished Masters thesis, Bank Street College of Education, New York, 1975.

Pettigrew, T. F. The measurement and correlation of category width as a cognitive variable. *Journal of Personality*, 1958, *26*, 532-544.

Pikas, A. *Abstraction and concept formation*. Cambridge, Massachusetts: Harvard University Press, 1966.

Reali, N., & Hall, V. Effect of success and failure on the reflective and impulsive child. *Developmental Psychology*, 1970, *3*, 392-402.

Reichard, S., Schneider, M., & Rapaport, D. The development of concept formation in children. *American Journal of Orthopsychiatry*, 1944, *14*, 156-161.

Ricciuti, H. N. Object grouping and selective ordering behavior in infants 12 to 24 months old. *Merrill-Palmer Quarterly*, 1965, *11*, 129-148.

Riegel, K. F. Dialectical operations: The final period of cognitive development. *Human Development*, 1973, *16*, 346-370.

Rosch, E. Natural categories. *Cognitive Psychology*, 1973, *4*, 328-350.

Rosch, E. Universals and cultural specifics in human categorization. In R. Brislin, S. Bochner, & W. Lonner (Eds.), *Cross-cultural perspectives on learning*. New York: Sage/ Halsted, 1974.

Rozelle, R. M., & Campbell, D. T. More plausible rival hypotheses in the cross-lagged panel correlational technique, *Psychological Bulletin*, 1969, *71*, 74-80.

Ruble, D. N., & Nakamura, C. Y. Task orientation versus social orientation in young children and their attention to relevant social cues. *Child Development*, 1972, *43*, 471-480.

Salkind, N. Errors and latency on the MFFT: A reassessment of classification strategies. Paper presented at the Biennial Meeting of the Society for Research in Child Development, Denver, April 1975.

Saltz, E. *The cognitive bases of human learning.* Homewood, Illinois: Dorsey, 1971.

Saltz, E., & Sigel, I. E. Concept overdiscrimination in children. *Journal of Experimental Psychology*, 1967, *73*, 1-8.

Saltz, E., Soller, E., & Sigel, I. E. The development of natural language concepts. *Child Development*, 1972, *43*, 1191-1202.

Santostefano, S. G. A developmental study of the cognitive control "leveling-sharpening." *Merrill-Palmer Quarterly*, 1964, *10*, 343-360.

Santostefano, S. G., & Paley, E. Development of cognitive controls in children. *Child Development*, 1964, *35*, 939-949.

Schacter, F., Cooper, A., & Gordet, R. A method for assessing personality development for follow-up evaluation of the preschool child. *Monographs of the Society for Research in Child Development*, 1968, *33*(3, Serial No. 119).

Schleifer, M., & Douglas, V. I. Moral judgements, behaviour, and cognitive style in young children. *Canadian Journal of Behavioral Science*, 1973, *5*, 133-144.

Sherman, J. A. Problem of sex differences in space perception and aspects of intellectual functioning. *Psychological Review*, 1967, *74*, 290-299.

Shipman, V. C. *Structural stability and change in the test performance of urban preschool children.* (PR-72-18) Princeton, New Jersey: Educational Testing Service, 1972.

Siegel, A. W., Kirasic, K. C., & Kilburg, R. R. Recognition memory in reflective and impulsive preschool children. *Child Development*, 1973, *44*, 651-656.

Sigel, I. E. Developmental trends in the abstraction ability of children. *Child Development*, 1953, *24*, 131-144.

Sigel, I. E. *SCST manual: Instructions and scoring guide.* Detroit: Merrill–Palmer Institute, 1967.

Sigel, I. E. The development of classificatory skills in young children: A training program. In W. W. Hartup (Ed.), *The young child: Review of research.* Vol. 2. Washington, D. C.: National Association for the Education of Young Children, 1972.

Sigel, I. E., Anderson, L. M., & Shapiro, H. Categorization behavior of lower- and middle-class Negro preschool children: Differences in dealing with representation of familiar objects. *Journal of Negro Education*, 1966, *35*, 218-229.

Sigel, I. E., Jarman, P., & Hanesian, H. Styles of categorization and their intellectual and personality correlates in young children. *Human Development*, 1967, *10*, 1-17.

Sigel, I. E., & McBane, B. Cognitive competence and level of symbolization among five-year-old children. In J. Hellmuth (Ed.), *The disadvantaged child.* Vol. 1. New York: Brunner-Mazel, 1967.

Sigel, I. E., & Olmsted, P. Modification of cognitive skills among lower-class black children. In J. Hellmuth (Ed.), *The disadvantaged child,* Vol. 3. New York: Brunner-Mazel, 1970.

Siegelman, E. Reflective and impulsive observing behavior. *Child Development*, 1969, *40*, 1213-1222.

Signell, K. A. Cognitive complexity in person perception and nation perception: A developmental approach. *Journal of Personality*, 1966, *34*, 517-537.

Singer, S. S., & Weller, L. Classification patterns of underpriviledged children in Israel. *Child Development*, 1971, *42*, 581-594.

Smock, C. D. The influence of psychological stress on the "intolerance of ambiguity." *Journal of Abnormal and Social Psychology*, 1955, *50*, 177-182.

Stanes, D. Analytic responses to conceptual style test as a function of instructions. *Child Development*, 1973, *44*, 389-391.

Stott, L., & Ball, R. S. Infant and preschool mental tests: Review and evaluation. *Monographs of the Society for Research in Child Development*, 1965, *30*(3, Serial No. 101).

Switzky, H. N., Haywood, H. C., & Isett, R. Exploration, curiosity, and play in young children: Effects of stimulus complexity. *Developmental Psychology*, 1974, *10*, 321-329.

Thurstone, L. L., & Thurstone, T. G. *Primary mental abilities.* Chicago: Science Research Associates, 1963.

Vaught, G. M., Pittman, M. D., & Roodin, P. A. Developmental curves for the portable rod-and-frame test. *Bulletin of the Psychonomic Society*, 1975, *5*, 151-152.

Vernon, P. E. The distinctiveness of field independence. *Journal of Personality*, 1972, *40*, 366-391.

Vernon, P. E. Multivariate approaches to the study of cognitive styles. In J. R. Royce (Ed.), *Multivariate analysis and psychological theory*. New York: Academic Press, 1973.

Vurpillot, E. The development of scanning strategies and their relation to visual differentiation. *Journal of Experimental Child Psychology*, 1968, *6*, 632-650.

Vygotsky, L. *Thought and language.* Cambridge, Massachusetts: MIT Press, 1962.

Wachtel, P. L. Style and capacity in analytic functioning. *Journal of Personality*, 1968, *36*, 202-212.

Wachtel, P. L. Cognitive style and style of adaptation. *Perceptual and Motor Skills*, 1972, *35*, 779-785.   (a)

Wachtel, P. L. Field dependence and psychological differentiation: Re-examination. *Perceptual and Motor Skills*, 1972, *35*, 179-189.   (b)

Wallach, M. A., & Caron, A. J. Attribute criteriality and sex-linked conservatism as determinants of psychological similarity. *Journal of Abnormal and Social Psychology*, 1959, *59*, 43-50.

Wallach, M. A., & Kogan, N. *Modes of thinking in young children.* New York: Holt, Rinehart & Winston, 1965.

Ward, W. C. Creativity in young children. *Child Development*, 1968, *39*, 737-754.   (a)

Ward, W. C. Reflection-impulsivity in kindergarten children. *Child Development*, 1968, *39*, 867-874.   (b)

Ward, W. C. *Correlates and implications of self regulatory behaviors.* (PR-73-42) Princeton, New Jersey: Educational Testing Service, 1973.   (a)

Ward, W. C. *Development of self regulatory behaviors.* (PR-73-18.) Princeton, New Jersey: Educational Testing Service, 1973.   (b)

Wechsler, D. *Wechsler Intelligence Scale for Children.* New York: The Psychological Corporation, 1949.

Wechsler, D. *Manual for the Wechsler Preschool and Primary Scale of Intelligence.* New York: The Psychological Corporation, 1967.

Weisz, J. R. O'Neill, P., & O'Neill, P. C. Field dependence-independence on the Children's Embedded Figures Test: Cognitive style or cognitive level? *Developmental Psychology*, 1975, *11*, 539-540.

Werner, H. The concept of development from a comparative and organismic point of view. In D. B. Harris (Ed.), *The concept of development: An issue in the study of human behavior.* Minneapolis: University of Minnesota Press, 1957.

White, K. M. Conceptual style and conceptual ability in kindergarten through the eighth grade. *Child Development*, 1971, *42*, 1652-1656.

Wilson, C. D., & Lewis, M. *Temperament: A developmental study in stability and change during the first four years of life.* (RB-74-3) Princeton, New Jersey: Educational Testing Service, 1974.

Witkin, H. A. Origins of cognitive style. In C. Scheerer (Ed.), *Cognition: Theory, research, promise.* New York: Harper & Row, 1964.

Witkin, H. A. *The role of cognitive style in academic performance and in teacher-student relations.* (RB-73-11.) Princeton, New Jersey: Educational Testing Service, 1973.

Witkin, H. A. & Berry, J. W. Psychological differentiation in cross cultural perspective. *Journal of Cross-Cultural Psychology*, 1975, *6*, 4-87.

Witkin, H. A., Dyk, R. B., Faterson, H. F., Goodenough, D. R., & Karp, S. A. *Psychological differentiation.* New York: Wiley, 1962.

Witkin, H. A., Goodenough, D. R., & Karp, S. A. Stability of cognitive style from childhood to young adulthood. *Journal of Personality and Social Psychology*, 1967, 7, 291-300.

Witkin, H. A., Lewis, H. B., Hertzman, M., Machover, K., Meissner, P. B., & Wapner, S. *Personality through perception.* New York: Harper & Row, 1954.

Witkin, H. A., Oltman, P. K., Raskin, E., & Karp, S. A. *A manual for the Children's Embedded Figures Test.* Palo Alto, California: Consulting Psychologists Press, 1971.

Wohlwill, J. F. *The study of behavioral development.* New York: Academic Press, 1973.

Wright, J. C. *The Kansas Reflection Impulsivity Scale for Preschoolers (KRISP).* St. Louis: CEMREL, Inc., 1971.   (a)

Wright, J. C. Reflection-impulsivity and associated observing behaviors in preschool children. Paper presented at the Biennial Meeting of the Society for Research in Child Development, Minneapolis, April 1971.   (b)

Wright, J. C. *Technical report on the Kansas Reflection-Impulsivity Scale for Preschoolers (KRISP).* Lawrence, Kansas: Kansas Center for Research in Early Childhood Education, 1972.

Wright, J. C. *A users' manual for the KRISP.* St. Louis: CEMREL, Inc., 1973.

Wright, J. C. Reflection-impulsivity and information processing from three to nine years of age. Paper presented at the 82nd Annual Convention of the American Psychological Association, New Orleans, September, 1974.

Yando, R. M., & Kagan, J. The effect of task complexity on reflection-impulsivity. *Cognitive Psychology*, 1970, *1*, 192-200.

Zelniker, T., Jeffrey, W. E., Ault, R., & Parsons, J. Analysis and modification of search strategies of impulsive and reflective children on the Matching Familiar Figures Test. *Child Development*, 1972, *43*, 321-335.

Author Index

Numbers in *italics* refer to pages on which the complete references are listed.

Subject Index